TY COBB

TY COBB

A BIOGRAPHY

DAN HOLMES

BASEBALL'S ALL-TIME GREATEST HITTERS

GREENWOOD PRESS
WESTPORT, CONNECTICUT • LONDON

Library of Congress Cataloging-in-Publication Data

Holmes, Dan.
    Ty Cobb : a biography / Dan Holmes.
        p. cm.—(Baseball's all-time greatest hitters)
    Includes bibliographical references and index.
    ISBN 0–313–32869–2 (alk. paper)
    1. Cobb, Ty, 1886–1961.   2. Baseball players—United States—Biography.   I. Title.   II.
Series.
    GV865.C6H65   2004
    796.357'092—dc22   2004054370
    [B]

British Library Cataloguing in Publication Data is available.

Library of Congress Catalog Card Number: 2004054370
ISBN: 0–313–32869–2

First published in 2004

Greenwood Press, 88 Post Road West, Westport, CT 06881
An imprint of Greenwood Publishing Group, Inc.
www.greenwood.com

Printed in the United States of America

The paper used in this book complies with the
Permanent Paper Standard issued by the National
Information Standards Organization (Z39.48–1984).

10 9 8 7 6 5 4 3 2 1

I DEDICATE THIS BOOK TO THE SPECIAL WOMEN IN MY LIFE: MY SUPPORTIVE GRANDMOTHER, JANE; MY LOVING MOTHER, BEVERLY; MY BEAUTIFUL WIFE, KATE; AND MY DAUGHTERS ADRIENNE AND ELLERY, THE GREATEST THINGS TO EVER HAPPEN TO ME.

CONTENTS

SERIES FOREWORD

The volumes in Greenwood's "Baseball's All-Time Greatest Hitters" series present the life stories of the players who, through their abilities to hit for average, for power, or for both, most helped their teams at the plate. Much thought was given to the players selected for inclusion in this series. In some cases, the selection of certain players was a given. **Ty Cobb**, **Rogers Hornsby**, and **Joe Jackson** hold the three highest career averages in baseball history: .367, .358, and .356, respectively. **Babe Ruth**, who single-handedly brought the sport out of its "dead ball" era and transformed baseball into a home-run hitters game, hit 714 home runs (a record that stood until 1974) while also hitting .342 over his career. **Lou Gehrig**, now known primarily as the man whose consecutive-games record Cal Ripken Jr. broke in 1995, hit .340 and knocked in more than 100 runs eleven seasons in a row, totaling 1,995 before his career was cut short by ALS. **Ted Williams**, the last man in either league to hit .400 or better in a season (.406 in 1941), is widely regarded as possibly the best hitter ever, a man whose fanatical dedication raised hitting to the level of both science and art.

Two players set career records that, for many, define the art of hitting. **Hank Aaron** set career records for home runs (755) and RBIs (2,297). He also maintained a .305 career average over twenty-three seasons, a remarkable feat for someone primarily known as a home-run hitter. **Pete Rose** had ten seasons with 200 or more hits and won three batting titles on his way to establishing his famous record of 4,256 career hits. Some critics have claimed that both players' records rest more on longevity than excellence. To that I would say there is something to be said about longevity and, in both cases, the player's excellence was the reason why he had the opportunity to keep playing, to keep tallying hits for his team. A base hit is the mark of a successful plate appearance; a home run is the apex of an at-bat. Accordingly, we could hardly have a series titled "Baseball's All-Time Greatest Hitters" without including the two men who set the career records in these categories.

Joe DiMaggio holds another famous mark: fifty-six consecutive games in which he obtained a base hit. Many have called this baseball's most unbreakable record. (The player who most closely approached that mark was Pete Rose, who hit safely in forty-four consecutive games in 1978.) In his thirteen seasons, DiMaggio hit .325 with 361 home runs and 1,537 RBIs. This means he *averaged* 28 home runs and 118 RBIs per season. MVPs have been awarded to sluggers in various years with lesser stats than what DiMaggio achieved in an "average" season.

Because **Stan Musial** played his entire career with the Cardinals in St. Louis—once considered the western frontier of the baseball world in the days before baseball came to California—he did not receive the press of a DiMaggio. But Musial compiled a career average of .331, with 3,630 hits (ranking fourth all time) and 1,951 RBIs (fifth all time). His hitting prowess was so respected around the league that Brooklyn Dodgers fans once dubbed him "The Man," a nickname he still carries today.

Willie Mays was a player who made his fame in New York City and then helped usher baseball into the modern era when he moved with the Giants to San Francisco. Mays did everything well and with flair. His over-the-shoulder catch in the 1954 World Series was perhaps his most famous moment, but his hitting was how Mays most tormented his opponents. Over twenty-two seasons the "Say Hey Kid" hit .302 and belted 660 home runs.

Only four players have reached the 600-home-run milestone: Mays, Aaron, Ruth, and **Barry Bonds**, who achieved that feat in 2002. Bonds, the only active player included in this series, broke the single-season home-run record when he smashed 73 for the San Francisco Giants in 2001. In the 2002 National League Championship Series, St. Louis Cardinals pitchers were so leery of pitching to him that they walked him ten times in twenty-one plate appearances. In the World Series, the Anaheim Angels walked him thirteen times in thirty appearances. He finished the Series with a .471 batting average, an on-base percentage of .700, and a slugging percentage of 1.294.

As with most rankings, this series omits some great names. Jimmie Foxx, Tris Speaker, and Tony Gwynn would have battled for a hypothetical thirteenth volume. And it should be noted that this series focuses on players and their performance within Major League Baseball; otherwise, sluggers such as Josh Gibson from the Negro Leagues and Japan's Sadaharu Oh would have merited consideration.

There are names such as Cap Anson, Ed Delahanty, and Billy Hamilton who appear high up on the list of career batting average. However, a number of these players played during the late 1800s, when the rules of baseball were drastically different. For example, pitchers were not allowed to throw overhand until 1883, and foul balls weren't counted as strikes until 1901 (1903 in the American League). Such players as Anson and company undeniably were the stars of their day, but baseball has evolved greatly since then, into a game in which hitters must now cope with night games, relief pitchers, and split-fingered fastballs.

Ultimately, a list of the "greatest" anything is somewhat subjective, but Greenwood offers these players as twelve of the finest examples of hitters throughout history. Each volume focuses primarily on the playing career of the subject: his early years in school, his years in semi-pro and/or minor league baseball, his entrance into the majors, and his ascension to the status of a legendary hitter. But even with the greatest of players, baseball is only part of the story, so the player's life before and after baseball is given significant consideration. And because no one can exist in a vacuum, the authors often take care to recreate the cultural and historical contexts of the time—an approach that is especially relevant to the multidisciplinary ways in which sports are studied today.

Batter up.

ROB KIRKPATRICK
GREENWOOD PUBLISHING

ACKNOWLEDGMENTS

In telling the story of Ty Cobb's life, I relied on the files and scrapbooks of the National Baseball Hall of Fame Library; newspaper accounts; previously published biographies; the archives of the *Sporting News*; Cobb's personal diary; the Ty Cobb Museum in Royston, Georgia; and the Ernie Harwell Collection at the Detroit Public Library. I also consulted the files of Retrosheet, a grassroots organization working to compile every box score in baseball history. I am indebted to my friend Bill Burdick of the Hall of Fame for his assistance in obtaining photos. In addition, I must thank my colleague and accomplished author, Bruce Markusen, for recruiting me for what is my first book. I also owe a nod of thanks to every one of my fellow staff members at the Hall of Fame, who have helped me either directly or indirectly on this project.

This book is in part dedicated to everyone with whom I have ever watched a baseball game, and also to a few special people: to the memory of my great-grandfather Jacob Evink, an immigrant farmer from the Netherlands, who came to America in 1902, learned to love the game of baseball, and was buried with the transistor radio on which he listened to Tiger games; to my uncle Bob Hoyt, who gave me all his baseball cards; and to my father Dave Holmes, who served his country proudly for twenty years and taught me how a real man is supposed to conduct himself.

It is also dedicated to the memory of Tyrus Raymond Cobb, a man named for a city in Lebanon that wouldn't give up in the face of adversity, and who exhibited that same philosophy as the greatest player in the history of America's national pastime.

CHRONOLOGY

1886   Born Tyrus Raymond Cobb in the Narrows, Georgia, on December 18.

1893   Cobb's family moves to Royston, Georgia, where his father, William Herschel Cobb, takes a teaching job.

1897   At the age of 10, Cobb plays for his first baseball team, the Royston Rompers.

1901   At the age of 14, Cobb earns a promotion to the Royston Reds, playing with and against boys three to ten years older than he is.

1904   Cobb leaves home to play for the Augusta Tourists of the South Atlantic League. He is quickly released, but latches on with a professional team in Anniston, Alabama. He plays his first professional game on May 16. After the Anniston team folds later that year, Cobb's contract is purchased by Augusta. He plays for Augusta for the rest of the 1904 season, and begins the 1905 campaign there.

1905   On August 8, Cobb's father is killed by his mother in a shooting accident at their home in Royston, Georgia. On August 19, Cobb's contract is purchased by the Detroit Tigers. He reports to the Tigers on August 30, and makes his major league debut that day, collecting his first hit.

1906   Cobb's mother is acquitted on charges of voluntary manslaughter in the death of her husband.

1907   Cobb wins his first batting title and leads the Detroit Tigers to the American League pennant.

1908   On August 4, Cobb marries Charlotte Lombard in Augusta, Georgia.

1909   Cobb wins his third consecutive batting title, and the Tigers earn their third straight pennant, but also lose the World Series for the third time.

1911   Cobb wins his fifth straight batting title and enjoys his greatest season, batting .420 with an American League record 248 hits and 147 runs scored.

1915   Cobb sets a major league record with 96 stolen bases, and wins his ninth consecutive batting title.

1918   With the United States at war in Europe, Cobb reports for duty with the Chemical Warfare Service in New York City on October 1. A few weeks later, Lt. Cobb sails to Europe, where he serves for less than a month before the war ends on November 11.

1920   On December 18, his 34th birthday, Cobb is named manager of the Detroit Tigers, signing a $35,000 contract, the largest in baseball.

1925   After telling reporters that he would try to hit home runs for the first time in his career, Cobb slugs three home runs in St. Louis on May 5, setting a league record for total bases in one game. The next day, he blasts two more homers before returning to his base-hitting style of play.

1926   After six seasons as their manager, Cobb resigns from the Detroit Tigers and announces his retirement from baseball on November 4. On December 21, he is implicated in a gambling scandal with Tris Speaker and Joe Wood. The following spring, the charges are dropped.

1927   In February, Cobb returns from his brief retirement and signs a contract with Connie Mack's Philadelphia A's. In July he collects the 4,000th hit of his career.

1928   In his 24th and final major league season, Cobb hits .323 for the A's. He retires with the highest batting average in baseball history, as well as the most hits, runs scored, RBIs, and games played.

1936   Cobb is among five players elected to the Baseball Hall of Fame by baseball writers. He receives 222 votes, more than any other player, including Babe Ruth.

1939 On June 12, Cobb, along with the other inductees from the first four years of voting, are recognized in a ceremony at the newly opened National Baseball Hall of Fame and Museum in Cooperstown, New York.

1947 Cobb and his wife Charlotte are divorced.

1949 Cobb marries his second wife, Frances Fairburn, of Buffalo, New York. Their marriage ends in divorce in 1956.

1950 Wealthy from his investments in Coca-Cola, General Motors, and other stocks, Cobb contributes $100,000 for the creation of the Cobb Memorial Hospital in Royston, Georgia.

1961 On July 17, a 74-year-old Ty Cobb dies at a hospital in Atlanta. Later that year, his autobiography, *Ty Cobb: My Life in Baseball*, is released.

1962 Maury Wills breaks Cobb's record for most stolen bases during a season.

1969 Cobb is selected the greatest player in Detroit Tigers history in balloting by fans.

1977 Lou Brock breaks Cobb's career stolen base record.

1986 Pete Rose eclipses Cobb's career hits record.

1994 The motion picture *Cobb*, which portrays Cobb's final few months of life, is released. It features Tommy Lee Jones in the title role. A dark film that portrays Cobb in a negative light, it proves unsuccessful at the box office.

1999 Cobb is selected as a member of the All-Century Team by Major League Baseball.

INTRODUCTION

Ty Cobb played baseball with an unyielding passion. From the batter's box he studied each opposing pitcher, calculating and exploiting their weaknesses. On the bases, he attacked each ninety feet of the basepath with intensity, often steamrolling those who dared get in his way. He knew only one speed—full-throttle—and he maintained his feverish pace for twenty-four seasons until he owned nearly every mark in the baseball record book. As a consequence of his aggressive, competitive nature, Cobb made enemies in baseball, alienating teammates and opponents with his abrasive manner.

However, had it not been for that abrasive manner, history may have never taken account of Ty Cobb, and his name may have never risen to the heights it did. Even though he was blessed with athletic skill, and stood 6'0" and weighed a sleek 190 pounds in his prime, Cobb relied more on his brain than his physical attributes, regardless of the consequences. As Alan H. Levy wrote in his book *Rube Waddell*, "Cobb's contribution involved making the game more scientific, but hardly more civil."[1]

Cobb's will to succeed, instilled in him by his father, was the fuel that drove him to the top of the baseball mountain. He was never satisfied with being good. He needed to be the best. The death of his father when Cobb was 17 years old had a profound impact on Cobb's psyche, though not in quite the demonic way that some writers have suggested over the years. Yes, his father's death (in an accidental shooting by his mother), scarred Cobb, but whether or not it led to his intense style of play on the diamond is debatable.

Ty Cobb was stubborn and driven before his father died, and he remained that way all his life. But he also possessed a southern gentleman's charm and a generous side that he displayed on many occasions. Sportswriter Bob Broeg wrote that "Ty was a man of incongruities—mean and kind, stingy and generous."[2] Contrary to many accounts, Cobb did have several friends in baseball, many of whom he stayed in touch with for several years. Cobb was more than just "mean-spirited." He was also bold, literate, confident, savvy, and cultured. He was baseball's first millionaire, a level of wealth he reached through several shrewd business decisions. He was one of the first players who realized that baseball was a business, and he demanded compensation to ensure his future as well as that of his family. On more than one occasion, Cobb was prepared to walk away from baseball if he didn't receive the compensation he felt he deserved.[3]

When Cobb retired in 1928, he was generally considered the greatest player of all time. He had played in more games, collected more hits, scored more runs, and stolen more bases than any player in baseball history. Amazingly, 45 years later, all those records were still in place. It was impossible to convince anyone who had seen him play that anyone was better. "He did everything except steal first base. And I think he even did that in the dead of night," said pitcher Rube Bressler of Cobb.[4] George Sisler, a Hall of Fame first baseman who played against Cobb for thirteen seasons, said, "The greatness of Ty Cobb was something that had to be seen, and to see him was to remember him forever."[5] According to Hall of Fame second baseman Charlie Gehringer, who played for Cobb, "Every time at-bat for him was a crusade, and that's why he's off in a circle by himself."[6]

In his final season, at the age of 41, with his legs suffering from years of slides and daring dashes around the bases, Cobb hit .323 to leave his all-time batting average resting at a remarkable .367 mark. No player since has ever approached that level of batting mastery. In fact, since Cobb retired in 1928, just thirty-one players have exceeded Cobb's lifetime batting average in any one single season.[7]

Cobb's legacy was much larger than the baseball record books. He was a wildly successful businessman and philanthropist after his playing career ended. Cobb was regarded as the most brilliant batter in history, and dozens of players sought his advice, including Ted Williams and Stan Musial. Several times after his playing days ended, Cobb was asked to visit teams in training camp and offer batting tips, which he did with great pride and a sense of responsibility.

Over the years, in both print and film, Cobb's life has been immortalized. As a consequence, to many, Cobb's incessant battles with teammates and opponents, and his bigotry toward blacks, have earned him a reputation as nothing more than a violent racist. Due to the focus on a few incidents, Cobb has emerged as a flat caricature instead of as the complex man that he was. In rural

Georgia, near the spot where he was born, Cobb's generosity has helped thousands of young people earn a college education, and the people surrounding Cobb's hometown of Royston have benefited from the hospital he built there.

Admittedly, throughout his life, Cobb carried with him prejudices and character flaws that resulted in broken friendships, failed marriages, and violent episodes. In one celebrated incident, Cobb vaulted into the stands and beat a man who was missing all the fingers on one hand and three fingers on the other. But to paint Cobb with a broad brush fails to do him justice. Just before his death, Cobb wrote in his autobiography, "I find little comfort in the popular Cobb as a spike-slashing demon of the diamond with a wide streak of cruelty in his nature. The fights and feuds I was in have been steadily slanted to put me in the wrong."[8] This book, while striving to be as objective as possible, shows Cobb to be at least partially correct. Several incidents for which Cobb's legacy is still tainted were actually far more tame or complicated than have been previously reported. Indeed, Cobb owns blame for being a short-tempered, high-strung, impulsive man, but he also was a man of his era. In Cobb's time, baseball was played by tough men who were willing to scrap, claw, and fight to succeed. Cobb stood out in that era for his tremendous ability and success, as well as for the veracity of his feuds and on-field play. But he was by no means the only player to be involved in such episodes.[9]

Cobb was a genius on the baseball diamond because of one thing: his unshakable resolve. According to Moe Berg, Cobb "was an intellectual giant. He was the most fascinating personality I ever met in baseball. To him, a ball game wasn't a mere athletic contest. It was a knock-'em-down, crush-'em, relentless war. He was their enemy, and if they got in his way he ran right over them."[10] Berg was a graduate of Princeton, a U.S. spy in World War II, a man fluent in several languages, and a fifteen-year veteran of the major leagues. The intellectual Berg recognized in Ty Cobb was determined to find a way to defeat his opponents. It was, unfortunately, that same determination that also led Cobb to the grave as a somewhat bitter and lonely man.

The subject of Ty Cobb is special to me. Growing up in Michigan, I rooted for the Detroit Tigers and learned their history and tradition. Cobb, of course, is a large part of that Tiger tradition, and when I learned as a child that I shared my birthday with "The Georgia Peach," I was hooked. As a boy, I read as many books on baseball as I could find, including one of my all-time favorites, *The Tiger Wore Spikes* by John McCallum. In researching this biography of Ty Cobb, I have come to realize that several stories in McCallum's book were myth. But Cobb's greatness as a ball player was not a myth. Cobb, like all great men, was an intricate web of redeeming qualities and flaws.

NOTES

1. Alan H. Levy, *Rube Waddell: The Zany, Brilliant Life of a Strikeout Artist* (Jefferson, NC: McFarland and Company, 2000), 85.

2. Bob Broeg, *Superstars of Baseball: Their Lives, Their Loves, Their Laughs, Their Laments* (South Bend, IN: Diamond Communications, 1994), 45.

3. During his holdout prior to the 1908 season, Cobb said, "I was willing to walk away from the game if I had to. A college or military career was completely attractive to me." Ty Cobb, with Al Stump, *My Life in Baseball, the True Record* (New York: Doubleday and Company, 1961), 79.

4. *Sporting Life*, August 31, 1917, 7.

5. *Sporting News*, August 18, 1959, 11.

6. Donald M. Honig, *Baseball When the Grass Was Real: Baseball from the Twenties to the Forties Told by the Men Who Played It* (New York: Coward, McCann & Geoghegan, 1975), 42.

7. Since 1928, among those batters qualifying for the batting championship, the thirty-one players who exceeded Cobb's lifetime batting average in any one single season are Lew Fonseca, Babe Herman, Rogers Hornsby, Lefty O'Doul, Bill Terry, Lou Gehrig, Chuck Klein, Freddy Lindstrom, Al Simmons, Pie Traynor, Paul Waner, Babe Ruth, Arky Vaughan, Luke Appling, Earl Averill, Charlie Gehringer, Joe Medwick, Joe DiMaggio, Ted Williams, Harry Walker, Stan Musial, Rod Carew, George Brett, Wade Boggs, Tony Gwynn, Andres Galarraga, Jeff Bagwell, Larry Walker, Nomar Garciaparra, Todd Helton, and Barry Bonds.

8. Cobb, *My Life in Baseball*, 5.

9. Babe Ruth, Tris Speaker, and Rogers Hornsby also had fights with fans in the stands during their celebrated careers.

10. Nicholas Dawidoff, *The Catcher Was a Spy: The Mysterious Life of Moe Berg* (New York: Pantheon Books, 1994), 55.

EARLY YEARS

Tyrus Raymond Cobb was born and raised in the heart of the south, in a rural community of farms called the Narrows, located in Banks County, Georgia, just across from the South Carolina border, and resting at the foot of the southern tip of the Great Smoky Mountains. The countryside was filled with tall pines rooted in red clay, separated by small farming communities.

Both of Cobb's parents were of Scotch-Irish descent. Ty's father, William Herschel Cobb, was a college graduate who worked as the only teacher for a nearby school. Ty's mother, Amanda Chitwood, was the daughter of a prominent local family, and married the 20-year-old William Herschel Cobb when she was just 12 years old in 1883. In the 1880s, it was not uncommon for women at that young age to marry. Amanda's father, Caleb Chitwood, a successful cotton farmer, was impressed with young W. H. Cobb, and gave his blessing to the union.

Three years into their marriage, the Cobb's welcomed the birth of a son, Tyrus Raymond, on December 18, 1886. W. H. Cobb had chosen the name Tyrus as a tribute to the ancient city of Tyre, located in what is now Lebanon, in the Middle East. During the fourth century B.C., Alexander the Great had orchestrated an attack on the city, only to receive fierce resistance from local armies. Impressed with the courage of that city, Cobb found it a suitable name for his first-born child. Two years later a second son, Paul, was born, and in 1890, Amanda gave birth to her only daughter, Florence.

The land where Ty grew up in Georgia was still scarred by the Civil War, which had concluded just twenty-one years before his birth. Most farming families were barely surviving, but the Cobbs lived fairly well, thanks to W. H. Cobb's education and the influence of his Chitwood in-laws. Where other families in the region who worked as farmers were at the whim of the weather, Cobb's family had steady income and survived the seasonal hardships. After teaching in the small Georgia farming communities of Carnesville, Harmony Grove, and Lavonia, Ty's father moved his family in 1893 to Royston, Georgia, located in southern Franklin County. In Royston, W. H. Cobb served as principal of the local school, earning distinction for himself and his family. Royston was different from their other stops; more than 500 people lived in the town, and the farmland was fertile and plentiful. Ty's father purchased more than 100 acres of land and farmed it in the summer months when school was out. Young Ty, as the oldest child, worked with his father, but didn't enjoy the work. Ty wanted to spend more time with the other youth of Royston, playing ballgames and tramping through the many hills and woods of the area. But his father demanded that Ty work his share, believing that games and idle time would lead his son to trouble.

Ty's father was a serious man, who worked hard to provide for his family and believed deeply in education and family. "I believe, and I believe nothing more earnestly," W. H. Cobb once wrote, "that education is the cornerstone on which we build democracy." He taught Ty the history of the Cobb family, which went back to their ancestors in England, who had come to America in the early seventeenth century, settling in Virginia. He told Ty about Thomas Willis Cobb, who was the first Cobb to move to Georgia, and who earned the rank of colonel in the Revolutionary War; and of T. W.'s son, Thomas, who served three terms as a U.S. congressman, was U.S. senator from 1824 to 1828, and later gained distinction as a Superior Court judge in Georgia. Thomas even had a county named for him, not far from Atlanta. Ty especially enjoyed the stories of Thomas Reade Roots Cobb, a remarkably diverse man who had written books on law, founded the Lumpkin Law School at the University of Georgia, served as a delegate to the Confederate Provisional Congress (where he quite possibly penned the Confederate Constitution), and raised his own regiment of troops, "Cobb's Legion," whom he led into battle. T.R.R. Cobb eventually rose to the rank of general in the Confederate Army and was killed in December 1862 at the Battle of Fredericksburg in Virginia. To Ty's father, the Cobb name meant greatness, and it carried a status that each member of the family was meant to uphold. To Ty, the family stories of success and war heroism led him to question his menial jobs behind a mule on his father's farm. "I was a Cobb," he wrote later, "and stuck behind a mule that broke wind when the breeze was the wrong way. I resented it deeply."[1] Cobb felt certain he was destined to do something far greater than work the land.

In Royston, W. H. Cobb's investment in farmland paid off for the family. Within a few years, Ty's father was not only principal of the school (known as Professor

Cobb to locals), but was also mayor of Royston, founder and editor of the *Royston Record*, and the most respected figure in the region. Later, W. H. Cobb was elected state senator, and served as county school commissioner, where he continued to preach the importance of education. But for Ty, his father's success cast a long shadow. Ty felt he would never measure up to his father's expectations, and try as he might, he failed to produce the success in school that his father demanded. Subsequently, Ty felt distant from his father, whom he saw as a brilliantly gifted man, someone he could never be, at least academically or professionally.

While he was away attending to the business of the Franklin County Board of Education, of which he was president, W. H. Cobb wrote the following letter to his son on January 5, 1902:

Tyrus, Dear Boy—

The first snow of the year of account is down today. It is two inches I reckon. It is all of a round fine hail not a single feathery flake, some lodge on the limbs of the trees. Our wheat and oats stood the winter all right, wheat is up nicely. We are all snowed in today principally on account of the cold weather. Hardly a sound has been heard today. It is nearly six o'clock. I knew the past cold weather would furnish you with some fine scenery up there and I am glad you have been receptive of its austere beauty and solemn grandeur, as to color, sound, and picturesque contour or outline. That is a picturesque and romantic country with solitude enough to give nature a chance to be heard in the soul. The presence of man and the jargon of artificiality and show do not crowd out the grand aspect of God's handiwork among these everlasting hills covered with its primieval [sic] forest, nor hush the grand oratorios of the winds, nor check the rush of her living leaping waters.

To be educated is not only to be master of the printed page but be able to catch the message of the star, rock, flower, bird, painting and symphony. To have eyes that really see, ears that really hear, an imagination that can construct the perfect from a fragment. It is truly great to have a mind that can respond to and open the door of the soul to all the legions of thoughts and symbols of knowledge and emotions that the whole universe around us brings to us.

Be good and dutiful, conquer your anger and wild passions that would degrade your dignity and belittle your manhood. Cherish all the good that springs up in you. Be under the perpetual guidance of the better angel of your nature. Starve out and drive out the demon that lurks in all human blood and ready and anxious and restless to arise and reign.

Yours affectionately, W. H. Cobb[2]

There was one part of young Ty's life that gave him the taste of success that he craved. In Royston, like most communities across the country, the most popular diversion in the 1890s and early 1900s was baseball, which the youths played in pastures, fields, and sandlots. Baseball was so popular in Royston that there were two teams: the Reds, for the older and more talented players, and the Rompers, a youth team. Cobb first played organized baseball for the Rompers, at the age of 10, in the spring and summer of 1897. He played with the Rompers through the age of 14, until his skills earned him a rare look with the Reds, who were without their starting shortstop one Saturday afternoon. Cobb filled in, collected three hits, played flawlessly in the field, and never played for the Rompers again. With the Royston Reds at the age of 14, he competed against boys and men who were three to ten years older than him, yet he stood out as a solid ballplayer with unique skills. One of his teammates on the Reds was Stewart D. Brown, a pitcher, who became a lifelong friend. Together on the Reds, Cobb and Brown were proud of their resilience, despite their youthful age compared to their teammates and opponents. They playfully called themselves, "the little potatoes that were hard to peal [sic]."[3]

On the baseball field, Ty finally found an arena in which he could bring pride to the Cobb name. But his father was not a fan of baseball, and he let Ty know it. On several occasions, his father refused to allow Ty to play in games, demanding that his son work on the farm instead. Desperate to play baseball as much as he could, Ty appealed to his mother, whom he hoped would accept his passion for the game and explain it to his demanding father. But Ty's mother was only a little more sympathetic, and the battle between Ty and his father over the young boy's future was beginning.

W. H. Cobb hoped for a bright future for all his children, and he especially saw great things in his oldest son. He expected Ty to follow a path toward medical school, law school, or a military academy. He recognized that Ty was a gifted athlete, but he tried to turn that talent toward farm work instead of baseball. One summer, W. H. Cobb spent hours working with his oldest son, showing him how to plant and care for the crops. Ty learned the importance of managing a farm as a business and overseeing the hired help. The young Cobb came away from the experience closer to his father—it was the first time W. H. Cobb had spent that much time talking to him—but Ty also came to realize two things: first, he didn't enjoy the life of a farmer, and second, he knew his father would never approve of anything but perfection.

Ty was a bright student, and he performed adequately in school, but he never applied himself the way he could have. He remembered years later that his mind was filled with "notions of adventure and thrills"—luxuries he scarcely had the opportunity for in the rural atmosphere of Royston.[4] In addition, young Ty

Cobb grappled with what his mother called "fits of attitude." In the fifth grade, after the boys lost a spelling competition to the girls, Ty beat up the boy who missed a word and caused the embarrassing defeat. Similar incidents of temper throughout his childhood and adolescence illustrated Ty's impatience with failure. At an early age, Ty had a difficult time accepting other people's imperfections, and he was unable to tolerate the faults of his classmates. Later, Cobb explained his philosophy of competition: "I never could stand losing. Second place didn't interest me. I had a fire in my belly."[5] Ironically, his father's scrutiny of his own character and performance, while almost certainly the source for Ty's own impatience, grinded at Cobb, and drove him away from his father.

When Ty was 16 years old, his manager on the Royston Reds, Bob McCreary, convinced W. H. Cobb to allow his son to travel with the team on trips to surrounding towns for ballgames, occasionally as far as into South Carolina. Wearing the bright red uniforms of the Royston team, Ty began to establish himself as a premier player, banging out base hits and playing well in the field. On one occasion in Royston, after Ty snared a ball for the game-saving catch, the hometown crowd hurled coins on the field in appreciation. The affectionate response allowed Cobb to buy his first nice mitt and pair of spikes. Another man who supported Ty's baseball pursuits was Reverend John Yarborough, known in Royston as "Brother John." Yarborough had been Ty's Sunday school teacher (reportedly there had been a rule that all Royston Rompers were required to attend Sunday school to be eligible to play ball, and Ty never missed a session), was the assistant pastor of the Methodist Church, and served as a player-coach on the Reds. Yarborough recognized Ty's talents on the ballfield and supported the youngster in his play.

Each year throughout his teenage years, Ty would visit his relatives in North Carolina, often for weeks at a time, sometimes in the summer, and occasionally in the winter months. With his Chitwood relatives in North Carolina, Cobb indulged his baseball passion, walking or riding to nearby towns to play ball. His grandfather Caleb Chitwood was a strong influence on young Ty, taking him fishing, hunting, and hiking, pastimes that Cobb embraced throughout his life, and that he used to keep his lungs and legs strong for baseball.

It was about the age of 15 or 16 that Cobb adopted his trademark style of batting. Using what he called a "snap swing," Cobb would hold the bat with his hands apart and well up on the handle, allowing himself maximum control in attacking the ball. With his hands apart, Cobb was able to gauge the trajectory of the ball and adjust his hands depending on the location and whether he wanted to slap the ball, spray it to the opposite field, or hit it for distance. Later in his career, as players began to hold the bat at the end of the handle and simply slug for power all the time, Cobb stubbornly maintained that his method was preferable.

Playing ball for Royston from the ages of 14 to 16, Cobb stood out among his teammates and most of his opponents. Even at that early age, Cobb was larger than men four and five years his senior. At 5'10" and nearly 160 pounds, the 16-year-old Cobb was a speedster on the basepaths and had the strength to hit the ball into the outfield gaps. In the field, he used his speed to compensate for a lack of intuition, still playing some shortstop as well as center field for the Reds. His throwing arm was strong and accurate and he was beginning to learn the fine points of bunting and the hit-and-run play. In one contest against the Harmony Grove nine, Cobb laced a double over the left fielder's head, swiped third base easily, and scored on a bobbled ground ball after rattling the infielders with his cunning and aggressiveness. Later in his memoirs, Cobb would write of that period: "I was then quite a ball player for a boy who had never had any experience except in a little town. I had all the fundamentals. I could hit, run and field."[6] Apparently even Ty's father was impressed with his son's exploits, and the next day the *Royston Record* carried a front page story of the game.

But despite Ty's talents, his father still had his son aimed at a college education, and Ty was resigned to that course as well. He hoped that he could enter the University of Georgia after his prep schooling and find a spot on the university ball team. However, in the winter of 1903, a few well-placed letters turned those plans upside down and altered Cobb's life forever. Van Bagwell, a teammate of Ty's on the Royston Reds, had been given a tryout with the Nashville Volunteers of the Southern Association during a trip to Tennessee in the summer of 1903. Although he failed to make the team, Bagwell did strike up a friendship with Newt Fisher, the manager. He told Fisher that there were some players in southern Georgia who they may be interested in, including Cobb. When Cobb heard that, he was spellbound. He couldn't believe that someone thought he was professional material. He listened to Bagwell's stories of the professionals he'd met in Nashville and dreamed of the opportunity to play baseball for a living. Over several weeks in the winter of 1903, Cobb secretly mailed letters to all the teams in the newly formed South Atlantic League, which would play in Georgia, Florida, and South Carolina, beginning the following spring. In the letters, Cobb included general information about himself, as well as a few newspaper clippings of his baseball exploits. To his delight, one letter was answered by the owner of the Augusta club, Con Strouthers, who agreed to let Cobb come to spring training as long as he paid his own expenses. He guaranteed Cobb a salary of $50 a month if he made the team.

According to Cobb, the letter was a "bombshell" in the Cobb home. Although he had known of Strouthers' offer for weeks, Cobb waited to confront his father until the night before he was to report to Augusta. Sitting in W. H. Cobb's study, Ty listened as his father belittled the game of baseball and rampaged about the importance of an education. After several hours, seeing that Ty would not budge from his desire to go to Augusta, his father gave up the fight. He handed his son six checks each in the amount of $15 and told him to "get it out of your system."[7]

The next day, Cobb traveled by train to Augusta with his friend and Royston Reds teammate, Stewart Brown, to begin his quest for a professional baseball career. Just 17 years old, Cobb was the youngest player in camp, and it showed. In his first informal workout, Cobb romped in the outfield, cutting in front of the other players as they waited to catch pop flies, and drawing stares in his bright red Royston uniform. His exuberance stood out in the group of veteran ballplayers, most of whom were guaranteed a spot on the club. In the first game of the exhibition season, Strouthers played Cobb in center field due to a contract squabble with one of his players, Harry Bussey. Ty responded with a pair of hits, including a double, and scored two runs. The following day he was again in center, but after the game Strouthers called the youngster into his office and released him. Bussey had signed his contract and Cobb was no longer needed. Ty was crushed.

Back in his hotel room, Cobb dreaded the thought of returning home to his father. Thad Hayes, a pitcher, had been released earlier that day, and was packing his bags in his room when Cobb strolled by. He told Ty of the Anniston Noblemen, a team in the outlaw Tennessee-Alabama League that was looking for a few players. Outlaw leagues were not recognized by organized baseball, yet they flourished throughout the country at the time. He suggested that Cobb go with him to tryout for the Anniston club. When he made a phone call back home to his father, Cobb received the best news he could imagine. Rather than being angry, his father encouraged Ty to go after the job in Anniston. "It's unfortunate to be released after two days, but son, don't come home a failure."[8]

Buoyed by his father's words, Cobb arrived in Anniston, which lay halfway between Atlanta and Birmingham, Alabama. The league, which was not officially sanctioned by Organized Baseball, was created in response to the failure of the "Tri-State League," which had never gotten off the ground and which was to include teams from Alabama, Georgia, and Tennessee. Cobb and Hayes soon realized that they were more than qualified for the Anniston ballclub, which was comprised mostly of rejects and older men holding on to their ballplaying dreams. Anniston agreed to pay Cobb $65 a month, and also to pay for his room and board. Hayes received a similar deal. Cobb was assigned to live with a family by the name of Darden, who took good care of the young Georgian. At the time of Cobb's first professional baseball experience, he was a slender

5'10", weighing about 150 pounds. The 17-year-old had a fair complexion with a hawk nose and reddish-brown hair.

On the field, Cobb excelled, challenging for the league batting championship. Anxious to impress his family, Cobb sent clippings that heralded his feats on the field. But what Cobb really craved was the attention that would land him back in the pipeline to the big leagues. Cobb hatched a scheme to send clippings to Grantland Rice, the *Atlanta Journal*'s sports editor. Using assumed names, Cobb wrote letters to Rice, championing the "Cobb boy" in Anniston. In his biography, Cobb admitted he used "every type of handwriting I could manage" to fool Rice into believing the glowing reports were the work of several eyewitnesses. After some time, Rice surrendered to the barrage of "scouting reports" and mentioned Cobb in his baseball column. He wrote that word had reached Atlanta of a "young fellow named Cobb who seems to be showing an unusual lot of talent."[9] Cobb's talent caught more than the attention of Rice and his readers. With Anniston, Cobb hit nearly .300 in thirty-seven games and collected a league-best 9 triples before the league was shut down. His performance also caught the eye of his former employer; Augusta purchased his contract and brought him back to the South Atlantic League in early August.

Cobb was elated to be back in Augusta, and he was also glad to learn that Con Strouthers, the man who had released him early in the season, was no longer the Augusta manager. In his place was catcher Andy Roth, who saw Cobb's potential despite Ty's disappointing .237 average in thirty-seven late-season games with Augusta. Following the completion of the season, Roth offered Cobb a contract for 1905, hoping to wrap up the young outfielder as soon as possible. Cobb returned to Georgia and worked on his fathers' farm, mulling over his options for the next baseball season. His father was impressed that Ty had saved $200 during the season, and for the first time, he didn't quibble with his son's intentions to stick with baseball, despite his misgivings. W. H. Cobb still believed Ty's future should begin at the university or military academy. Unbeknownst to Ty was the fact that his father had saved a clipping from the *Atlanta Journal* praising his son's play and kept it tucked away in his vest pocket. Emboldened by his brimming confidence, Ty asked for $90 per month from the Augusta team, and after some correspondence, Roth agreed. Young Ty would play his first full professional season with the Augusta Tourists in 1905.

After training with the Detroit Tigers for the second straight spring, Augusta opened the 1905 season on April 19, with a team that had several talented ballplayers. They included George "Nap" Rucker, a strong-armed pitcher from Crabapple, Georgia, who later spent a decade in the National League with Brooklyn, winning 134 games. Joining Rucker on the mound was Eddie Cicotte (pronounced See-Cot), a knuckleball specialist from Michigan who became infamous in the 1919 Black Sox Scandal. The team also featured two friends from Dayton, Ohio, who both made it to the major leagues: pitcher Howie Holmes, whom everyone called "Ducky" after the outfielder of the same name who starred for several big league clubs in the 1890s and early 1900s; and burly Clyde Engle, a jack-of-all-trades whom Roth used as a catcher, but who made it to the big leagues as an outfielder-first baseman. Engle would be best known for being the man who hit the fly ball that the Giants Fred Snodgrass infamously muffed in the final game of the 1912 World Series between New York and the Red Sox. On a team populated with talent like this, Cobb began to blossom and learn his trade as a ballplayer.

In 1905, Cobb led the South Atlantic League (known as the Sally League) in batting average, hitting .326 in 103 games, with 60 runs scored and 40 stolen bases. Through trial and error, he had adopted a batting stance with his feet close together, near the back of the batters' box. Cobb held his hands a few inches apart on the bat handle, which allowed him to either slide his top left hand down to stroke for power, or move the bottom right hands up for a slap hit or bunt. Using that style, as he would his entire career, Cobb's 134 hits were the second-highest total in the league, trailing Paul Sentell, who would later play sixty-six games in the major leagues with an unimpressive .226 batting mark. By the middle of the season, Cobb was the most talented hitter in the league, and his average was more than eighty points higher than the norm for the loop. But in the outfield (playing mostly in left field at this point in his career), Ty showed his inexperience, committing 13 errors, the second most in the league. Despite his batting exploits, there were times when Cobb needed to be taken to task for his performance.

One of the crucial turning points in young Ty's professional playing career came in a game against Savannah during the 1905 season. Late in a close game, Cobb's new player-manager, George Leidy (who had replaced Roth in midseason), was shocked to see Cobb trot out to center field with a bag of popcorn in his hand. Determined to teach the young Cobb a lesson, Leidy left him in the game, hoping that an opportunity would arise for Ty to see the error of his ways. Soon enough it did—a lazy fly ball was hit in Cobb's direction. Drifting under it, Cobb tried to balance his snack and snare the ball, but was predictably unsuccessful. The ball bounced off his glove and a run scored. After the game, which Augusta won 2–1, Leidy gently chastised Cobb during a streetcar ride with his ballplayer. Leidy knew Ty had the talent to be a big leaguer, but he told the youngster that he would have to work at it and take the game seriously every day. Cobb would later say that the conversation with Leidy was a turning point.

"I made up my mind to be a big leaguer if it killed me. I never again thought of anything else while I was on the playing field. . . . Baseball, I knew all of a sudden, was my destiny."[10]

Following the popcorn episode in Savannah, Cobb practiced hard to make himself the best player on his team and ultimately in the Sally League. Leidy dedicated himself to helping Cobb hone his bunting skills, which would prove so valuable later in his big league career. "For hours, day after day, with an arm long since dead, he threw to me and I bunted. I bunted until I was worn out. Bit by bit, I got the knack of applying the bat squarely but with a withdrawing movement of the arms which softly placed the ball on or near the target."[11] Whereas Roth had tried to reign in Cobb's aggressive nature, Leidy worked to refine it and harness it. "My first help inside baseball came from Leidy—the reason I later made good in the majors was Leidy," Cobb recalled later in his autobiography. Years later, after Cobb was a star, he remembered Leidy by arranging for his old manager to secure a scouting position with Detroit.[12]

With Augusta in 1905, for the first time, Cobb began to have problems dealing with some of his teammates. Jealous of his success, some of Ty's teammates laughed and kidded him about his intensity. Although he had a good relationship with his roommate, Nap Rucker, an incident from the 1905 season illustrated Cobb's burning desire to excel. One day, in a home game against Charleston, Rucker was knocked off the mound after giving up several long hits. After the game, Cobb, as was customary, walked back to his room in his uniform, intent on taking his bath, as he always did. Because of his high-strung and impatient nature, Cobb always returned to the room before Rucker on game days, but on that day, Rucker was already nestled into the tub when Ty returned. Soon, Cobb was stomping mad outside the bathroom door, and Rucker hollered to see what was wrong. Cobb suddenly burst through the door, leapt at Rucker and began choking him. Rucker quickly shoved Cobb back and screamed at Cobb, "What's the matter with you, Ty? Are you crazy?" Cobb, still seething, replied, "You don't understand, Nap, I've just got to be the first—all the time." Cobb and Rucker's friendship survived the bathtub incident, and Rucker even played a part in Cobb's eventual success. During their time as teammates, Rucker, a lefty twirler, would throw extra batting practice to Cobb, so Ty could learn to hit southpaw pitching. Later, when Rucker won twenty-two games for Brooklyn in the National League, he credited his practice sessions with Cobb for strengthening his arm and teaching him to pitch to left-handed batters.

In early August, with Cobb's batting mark resting atop the South Atlantic League ledger, rumors began to surface that several players on the Augusta team were being scouted by major league clubs. Cobb knew that Cicotte was destined for the big leagues. In the spring, he had been given a trial by the Detroit Tigers, who trained in Augusta, and Detroit retained the right to pluck Cicotte off the Tourists' roster in return for a donation to the team's operation. What Cobb learned later in the season was that Detroit had also made an arrangement to buy any additional Augusta player for the humble price of $500. Speculation among the players was that Clyde Engle would be purchased, because he was a versatile performer able to man any of the infield or outfield slots. But given Cobb's batting feats, he was in the running as well. Early in August, Detroit scout Henry "Heinie" Youngman told Cobb that it was only a matter of time before he would be purchased by the Tigers and be up in the big leagues. Cobb's dream of playing at the major league level was imminent.

Amidst this great anticipation, Cobb received shocking news on the morning of August 9, 1905. His father had been killed in a shooting accident. Cobb immediately left the team and made his way back home to Royston, stunned that his father, the man he had tried so hard to please, was gone. He also realized that his dreams of baseball glory, however close they were to being realized, would never be shared with W. H. Cobb.

NOTES

1. Gene Schoor, *The Story of Ty Cobb, Baseball's Greatest Player* (New York: Messner, 1952), 19.

2. W. H. Cobb, letter to Ty Cobb, National Baseball Hall of Fame Library.

3. Schoor, *The Story of Ty Cobb*, 23.

4. Ibid., 27.

5. John McCallum, *The Tiger Wore Spikes: an Informal Biography of Ty Cobb* (New York: A.S. Barnes and Company, 1956), 16.

6. Ty Cobb, *Memoirs of Twenty Years in Baseball*, ed. William R. Cobb (self-published by William R. Cobb, 2002), 29.

7. Ty Cobb, with Al Stump, *My Life in Baseball*, 45.

8. Cobb, with Stump, *My Life in Baseball*, 47.

9. Ibid., 50.

10. Schoor, *The Story of Ty Cobb*, 38.

11. McCallum, *The Tiger Wore Spikes*, 31.

12. Cobb, with Stump, *My Life in Baseball*, 49.

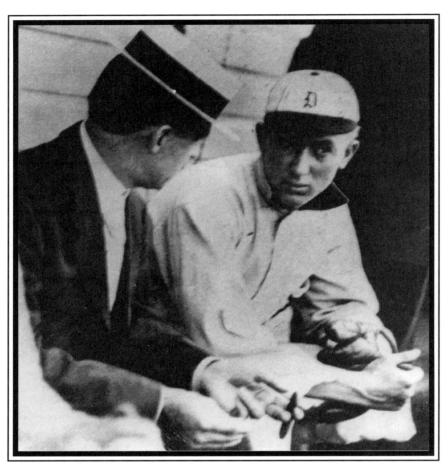

Ty Cobb on the bench with Bill Armour prior to Cobb's first Major League game. *National Baseball Hall of Fame Library, Cooperstown, N.Y.*

JEALOUSY AND PERSECUTION

When Ty Cobb arrived in Royston, Georgia, on August 10, 1905, his father was dead from a shotgun blast and his mother was facing arrest for involuntary manslaughter. The small community was abuzz over the shocking death of their most influential and prominent figure, while Ty was in a state of shock at the loss of his father.

It soon became apparent what had happened the evening of August 8 at the Cobb residence. Contrary to Cobb's description of a "shooting accident" in his autobiography, there was more to the story. Suspicious that his young, attractive wife was having an affair, W. H. Cobb had set a trap. Telling his wife that he was going out to their farm for a few days, he hitched his horse to his buggy, left their home, and made a plan to catch his wife in the arms of her lover. That night, as he quietly made his way back to his home, W. H. Cobb was seen walking in Royston alone. Shortly after midnight, he climbed to the top of the roof above his porch and crept to their bedroom window, finding it locked. Amanda Cobb was awakened by the sound of footsteps on the roof and retrieved a shotgun, which she kept within reach when she was left alone. According to the neighbors, two shots were fired, though not in quick succession. Amanda Cobb had shot her husband twice, once in the abdomen, and once in the head. Joe Cunningham, a neighbor and friend of Ty's, heard the shots and made his way to the Cobb residence. When he arrived, he found Amanda Cobb kneeling over her husband, who was still holding on to life, despite massive bleeding from a large hole in his stomach and from the side of his head. Cunningham called it "the worst thing I ever saw." A doctor was summoned, but W. H. Cobb was pronounced dead at 1:30 A.M.[1]

Despite her explanation that she had mistaken W. H. Cobb for an intruder, from the beginning Amanda Cobb was suspected of having murdered her husband. The authorities found a revolver in his pocket, and the testimony of eyewitnesses in Royston who had seen Mr. Cobb walking toward his home led them to speculate that the cause of death was a domestic squabble. On August 9, Amanda Cobb testified to a coroner's jury as to what had occurred. On August 11, with Ty and her other children at home, a funeral was held at the Cobb residence for William Herschel Cobb. The following day, the sheriff arrested Amanda Cobb and set her bail at $7,000, a portion of which she was able to post to receive her release.

Ty spent a week at home with his mother and two siblings before returning to Augusta to join the team. The fact that he wasted little time in returning to his playing career is an indication that Cobb desired to be away from the gossip of Royston and the overwhelming anguish of his father's death. Though he rarely spoke of his father's death the remainder of his life, Cobb was greatly affected in many ways. The suspicious circumstances of the death cast a dark cloud over his family's otherwise respectable name. It soon became evident that, before the shooting, many people in Royston had suspected that Amanda Cobb was having an affair, and it may have even been brought to W. H. Cobb's attention by a friend. At 33 years of age, Amanda Cobb was nearly twenty years younger than her husband, and she was described as "beautiful and radiant."[2] Eighteen-year-old Ty, though he was not close to his mother, didn't suspect her of wrongdoing, at least not outwardly. "This isn't the kind of people Cobbs are," he said at the time.[3]

Back with the Tourists, Cobb returned to the line-up on August 16, collecting two hits in the first game of a double-header against Charleston. Three days later, Charles D. Carr, the president of the Augusta club, informed Cobb that his contract had been purchased by the Tigers and that he would be expected to report to Detroit by the end of the month. The 18-year old Cobb was excited by the news but weakened by the thought that his father would never know of his accomplishment. Cobb played the next week for Augusta and appeared in his final game at home on August 25, in front of a large crowd. In the bottom of the first inning, as he made his way to the plate, Cobb was intercepted by several well-wishers, including the mayor of Augusta, who presented him with a watch and a bouquet of flowers. Cobb collected two hits in the game, stole a base, and recorded an assist from left field in his farewell to the Augusta faithful. His final average of .326 would stand up as the best mark in the league, and his 40 stolen bases ranked third. Though he was the youngest player on the Augusta team, Cobb would be the first to make it to the big leagues. Pitcher Eddie Cicotte would follow him a few days later, while Clyde Engle, Nap Rucker, and Ducky Holmes would make it in subsequent years.

After a brief stop back in Royston, Cobb was on his way north to Detroit. He had never been above the Mason-Dixon Line, and now he was on his way to a city larger than any he had ever seen. After a few missed connections, Cobb arrived in Detroit by train on August 29, and checked in to a hotel within walking distance of Bennett Park. Detroit's home stadium was located on the corner of Michigan and Trumbull in the heart of the city in a section called "Corktown" because of the predominance of Irish immigrants living there. Cobb reported to the park on the August 30, just over three weeks after the death of his father. He was ready to start his big league career. The *Detroit Free Press*, writing of his arrival and his minor league batting success, speculated that the young Georgian "wouldn't pile up anything like that in this league."[4]

Cobb saw action immediately with the Tigers, who were hosting the New York Highlanders in the second of a three-game series. Bennett Park was named for Charlie Bennett, a star for the National League's Detroit Wolverines in the 1880s. A catcher, Bennett's career was ended abruptly when he lost both of his legs in a terrible train accident in 1894. Bennett had been tremendously popular in Detroit, and in 1900, when the city earned a team in the Western League (later to become the American League), their ballpark was named in his honor.

The Highlanders, later to be known as the Yankees, started ace "Happy Jack" Chesbro, a master of the spit ball. The previous season, Chesbro had won an amazing forty-one games and pitched more than 400 innings for the New York club. The Tigers, managed by Bill Armour, countered with "Big George" Mullin, a fidgety right-hander from Wabash, Indiana. In front of an afternoon crowd of approximately 1,200 fans, Cobb hit fifth in the line-up, playing center field. Armour's Tigers, due to injury, had a shortage in the outfield. In the bottom of the first inning, the Tigers hit Chesbro hard, putting together a double, single, and a sacrifice bunt to plate one run and move another runner to third. With one out, the left-handed-hitting Cobb strolled to the plate for his first major league at-bat. Using the hands-apart grip that he'd perfected as a boy in Georgia, 18-year-old Ty Cobb peered out at Jack Chesbro and tried to overcome the nerves that were causing his stomach to twist and turn. The first pitch he saw was a high fastball that he swung through and missed. The next offering from Chesbro was a spitter that fooled Cobb for strike two. Chesbro then returned to his fastball, sending a pitch into the heart of the strike zone that Cobb met with a flick of his bat. The ball soared into the left, center-field gap for a hit. New York left fielder Frank "Noodles" Hahn's throw to second base was a split second too late to catch the sliding Georgian. Chris "Pinky" Lindsay, the Tigers runner on third, trotted home to make the score 2–0. Ty Cobb had his first hit in the big leagues, having victimized one of the best pitchers in the league. Though RBIs were not yet an official statistic, Cobb had driven in his first run. Ty walked against Chesbro his next time up, and with Sam Crawford in front of him on second base, Cobb was out on the back end of a double steal attempt, but it did little to dampen the day for the Tigers, as they vanquished the Highlanders 5–3. In center field, Cobb handled two put-outs without incident and his first big-league game was under his belt.

As impressive as his first game in the major leagues was, the fact that he was in a northern city on a strange team, with new teammates and a new manager, was nearly as impressive to young Ty. Bill Armour was in his first season as the manager of the Tigers, having previously managed Cleveland. Armour was a small, conservative man, who had never played professional baseball, and managed in a suit and tie, which was not uncommon in those days. Armour was four days shy of his thirty-sixth birthday, making him twice the age of the teenage Cobb. The Detroit manager was known for his trademark straw hat and his genial way with his team. Some complained that Armour was easily manipulated by his ballplayers, others simply called him "gentlemanly."[5] On the morning of Cobb's first game, Armour sat with the fresh-faced rookie and went over the details of his contract, which called for a salary of $1,500 for the year. Because he was reporting at the end of August, and would be with the team for a little over a month, Cobb would earn about $250. After Cobb penned his name to the contract, he changed into the heavy flannel uniform of the Detroit Tigers, which were white, trimmed in navy blue, and featured an old English "D" on the left breast. The team cap was white with a navy blue bill and stripes draping down from the button at the top, and an old English "D" on the front, also in blue.

The ballfield on which Cobb played his first major league game was larger than any he had ever seen, with a capacity of nearly 9,000, and grandstands wrapping around both the first and third base lines and reaching nearly to the foul poles. There were no seats in the outfield, though at times "wildcat bleachers" would be erected by zealous entrepreneurs hoping to make a buck. The game on the field was faster, and was played by men who were bigger, stronger, and more-skilled than any Cobb had ever seen. Whereas in the minor leagues Cobb had been one of the fastest players on the field, in the major leagues nearly every player was quick. Speed was paramount in the game of baseball in 1905. Baseball games were decided by pitching and defense. Runs were scarce. Teams fought to advance their runners from base to base and clawed to get a score across the plate. In 1905, the average American League team scored three-and-one-half runs per game, and pitchers posted a stingy 2.65 ERA. Teams relied on offensive pressure to force the defenders to make mistakes, which they did; AL clubs averaged nearly two errors per game.

As a southerner, Cobb was a rarity in the major leagues. In 1905, most ballplayers hailed from the northeast or the midwest; very few came from the deep south. Of Cobb's teammates on the 1905 Tigers, four were from Pennsylvania, three were from Illinois, two were from New York, two were from Massachussetts, two were from Ohio, two were from Michigan, two were from Indiana, two had been born in Canada, and only one had been born as far south as Missouri. To Cobb's teammates, Royston, Georgia must have seemed about as foreign to them as Norway—which was where right-hander Jimmy Wiggs was from. Furthermore, Cobb's teammates were of a different ideological persuasion than he was. More than half of his Detroit teammates were Irish Catholic, and they averaged ten years older than the young southern Baptist from Georgia. The next youngest player on the Detroit club was Charley O'Leary, the shortstop, who was in his second full major league campaign and four years older than Ty.

With these stark contrasts between Cobb and the rest of the Detroit club, Ty stood out among his teammates from the start. Some of his habits on the field caught their attention, as well. Since his days with the Royston Reds, Cobb had taken to swinging three bats while he waited on deck. When he approached the plate he discarded two of the bats and carried one piece of lumber, which felt lighter in his hands compared to the trio of sticks. His Tiger teammates had never seen anyone do this, and some of them took it as a cocky maneuver by Cobb. Left fielder Matty McIntyre disliked Ty from the very beginning, and the three-bat habit cemented his distrust of the fresh rookie from Georgia. On September 5, in the second game of a double-header against the Chicago White Sox in Detroit, a play in the outfield illustrated McIntyre's disdain for Cobb. Sox shortstop George Davis lofted a short fly to left-center-field. McIntyre trotted in to catch it, but Cobb darted in from center field and caught the ball. Had regular center fielder Duff Cooley (who was injured and out for the remainder of the season) made that play, McIntyre might not have flinched. But because it was Cobb who did it, McIntyre responded by chastising the rookie in the outfield, and he continued the barrage on the bench after the inning, further embarrassing Ty.

Notwithstanding McIntyre, Cobb did make friendships on the team, though they were few. Veteran players were generally distrustful of rookies, whom they saw as threats to their livelihood. But 39-year-old Bobby Lowe, in his sixteenth season in the big leagues, helped Cobb learn the ropes and even invited Ty to dine with he and his wife. Lowe played sparingly, but he used his years of experience to help Cobb and other young players on Detroit in both 1905 and

1906. A fine player in his prime, Lowe had starred for the Boston Beaneaters of the National League in the 1890s. The other Tiger who made an effort to befriend Cobb was pitcher Bill Donovan. Donovan, who earned the nickname "Wild Bill" more for the erratic control of his fastball than his lifestyle, was a bit of a loner on the team, but immensely popular with the Detroit partisans. He and Ty's friendship would last for several years.

With Cooley injured, Cobb settled in as the Tiger center fielder and played every game of the schedule after his arrival, nestled between nemesis McIntyre in left field and Sam Crawford, who barely acknowledged Ty, in right. When Cobb arrived, Detroit was in sixth place in the AL, fifteen and one-half games behind the league-leading Philadelphia Athletics. From that point on, the Tigers were the hottest team in the league, going 27–14 and crawling up to third place and a winning record for the season, at 79–74. Cobb's effort in those forty-one games—a .240 average with 7 extra-base hits and 19 runs scored—played a small part in the surging finish. On September 4, Cobb made his first spectacular defensive play, snaring a long fly ball with an over-the-shoulder grab against the White Sox. On September 12, in Detroit against Cleveland, Cobb beat out an infield hit in the ninth inning, and scored the winning run two batters later when he sprinted home on a deep grounder to second base. On September 23, Cobb collected the first home run of his career, circling the bases with an inside-the-park blow off Cy Falkenberg of the Washington Senators. Two teammates scored in front of Cobb on the play, which marked the first of his 46 career inside-the-park home runs—still a major league record. In an era when the outfield fences were deep and the ball traveled a shorter distance, a majority of the home runs hit in baseball were of the inside-the-park variety. Eventually, Cobb would become a master at accomplishing the feat.

The season concluded in Cleveland on October 7, the Tigers taking the game 7–1 behind Mullin. Following the return trip to Detroit, the team held an end of the season banquet, which Cobb attended, and most likely had his first taste of champagne. Throughout his playing career, Cobb rarely drank or smoked, except for an occasional puff of a pipe or sip of whiskey on his hunting trips.

Cobb left Detroit for Georgia the following day. What lay ahead was an agonizing off-season of uncertainty. His mother was still facing charges of involuntary manslaughter and Cobb expected to deal with her trial in the coming months. But when he arrived in Royston, Ty learned that the trial had been postponed until the following spring due to a heavy court docket. Working with his mother's attorneys, Ty helped craft her defense, while managing his family's farm with the help of his younger brother, Paul. As the oldest of the Cobb clan, and the only one earning a salary, Ty felt a weight on his shoulders. Even though he was to turn 19 years old that December, Cobb was very much a grown man with responsibilities. Apparently, at no time did Ty consider abandoning his career as a ballplayer to handle the Cobb farm full-time. For him, the death of his father not only cost him the most influential figure in his life, but it had severed the ties to W. H. Cobb's dreams of a military academy or college career for Ty. He would make his way as a baseball player and never look back.

In the off-season, Cobb worked on the Cobb farm and spent some leisure time in the woods, hunting with his dogs. In the early 1900s, there were no special training programs, diets, or workout schedules for baseball players. Many players reported to spring training each year in poor shape, having grown lazy in the off-season. Most importantly, they complained of "dead legs," which robbed a player of his quickness. Cobb would never allow himself to grow slow or overweight, which contributed to his long career. The heavy boots that he wore, and the packs that he carried with him on his hunting trips, helped strengthen his legs and his lungs. Over the winter of 1905–1906, Cobb grew a full inch and added 15 pounds to his wiry frame, all in muscle. His pastimes of hunting and hiking would serve him well throughout his career. At 6'0" and 170 pounds, Cobb would be one of the largest men on his team in 1906.

In January, Cobb received his contract from the Tigers, which was for $1,500. The letter from manager Bill Armour that accompanied the contract encouraged Ty to work on his bunting in the off-season and to report on time to spring training, which once again would be held in Augusta, Georgia. At some point that month, Cobb wrote Armour and asked permission to take a position coaching the Stone Mountain team, located just outside of Atlanta, and affiliated with the University of Georgia. Not hearing from Armour, Cobb took the position, and in February he traveled to Stone Mountain, where he worked with the young players, many of whom were just a few months younger than he was. On March 9, he reported to training, joining the Tigers in Augusta.[6]

Within days, Cobb's first spring training as a member of the Tigers was turning into a test of his mental resolve. A faction led by McIntyre began to ostracize Cobb, excluding him from batting practice, outfield warm-ups, and social events at the team hotel. Cobb ate his dinners alone, showered alone, and sat alone on their train trips to play exhibition games. At times he found his clothes ripped to shreds or burned in his hotel room, and his homemade bats were sawed into pieces on more than one occasion. McIntyre and his cronies locked Cobb out of the lone bathroom that the team shared on their floor at the Albion Hotel, forcing Cobb to take his showers at odd hours of the evening or early morning. Paranoid, Cobb began carrying a pistol, even to the ballpark.

The source of the harassment was three-fold. First, Cobb was a threat to earn a starting job over McIntyre and other veterans on the team. Second, he was considered a southern "hick" who was different from the rest of the team. Third, because he was a peculiarly nervous young man who seemed on edge all of the time, he was a perfect target for teasing. Sam Crawford, the best player on the Tiger team at that time, blamed the young Georgian for much of the problems: "Cobb came up with an antagonistic attitude, which in his mind turned any little razzing into a life-or-death struggle. He always figured everybody was ganging up on him."[7] To Cobb, who was already stressed over his mothers' impending trial, the treatment he received in the spring of 1906 was a nightmare.

Finally, after one particularly grueling day of torment, Cobb snapped. While practicing in the morning at Warren Park on an off-day in the exhibition schedule, Ty lashed out at his teammates, calling them "cowards" and challenging them to fight him. Shocked by the young man's tirade, most of the players laughed or backed away from the increasingly edgy Cobb. None took the challenge to fight him, which Cobb accepted as a sign of weakness. As the spring wore on, he withdrew further from the rest of the team. Unfortunately, Armour made no effort to bridge the widening gap between Cobb and his teammates, and unbeknownst to Ty, he actually encouraged ownership to trade the youngster. But no other major league team was interested in acquiring a high-strung, 19-year-old outfielder from Georgia who had hit .240 in his first trial in the league.

On March 30, Cobb went by train to Lavonia, Georgia, where his mother's criminal trial was beginning. When Cobb arrived his mother was on the stand reciting the details of the death of her husband. For the first time, Cobb heard in detail everything his mother had done that evening, and the next day other witnesses, including his friend Joe Cunningham, described the scene where W. H. Cobb lay dead at the window of his own bedroom, his head nearly blown off. Amanda Cobb explained that she had been terrified at the noises of someone trying to get into her bedroom. With all of her children away (Paul and Florence were staying with friends), she was alone in the home, scared for her life. According to newspaper accounts, the issue of whether or not Amanda Cobb was having an affair never arose. In addition, she was never asked why she locked the bedroom windows despite the fact that it had been a very warm evening. However, the chief prosecutor, S. J. Tribble, did confront her about the mystery of the two gunshots. Why had Mrs. Cobb fired one barrel of the shotgun, hit her target, and then fired several seconds later? Hadn't she recognized that she had shot her own husband?

Because all of the principles involved have long since died, the controversy of the gunshots will never be resolved, but for the members of the jury, all of whom were men, no controversy existed. After less than two hours of deliberation, on the afternoon of March 31, 1906, Amanda Chitwood Cobb was found not guilty of voluntary manslaughter. The Cobb name had been cleared.

Ty escorted his mother and siblings back to Royston, where he spent a few days with them before traveling with his brother Paul to Atlanta by train, where the younger Cobb was to attend Georgia Tech University. The following morning, Cobb joined his teammates in Birmingham, Alabama, where he played that afternoon in an exhibition game. Newspaper accounts make no mention of his mother's trial, but they do credit Ty with three hits in his first game back with the Tigers.

Within a week, Cobb had contracted a severe case of tonsillitis, most likely brought on by the travel and stress he had endured. Fearful that his malady might cause him his spot on the team, Cobb kept it to himself for days, continuing to play despite the pain. As the Tigers made their way north to start the season, stopping to play exhibition games as they went, Cobb found himself in Toledo, Ohio, when he could endure the pain no longer. With a fever over 102 degrees and a terrible pain in his throat that restricted him to eating soup, he finally went to a doctor. Teammate Herman "Germany" Schaefer, his roommate, went with Ty to see the physician. Over the course of three days, Cobb sat in shifts at the doctor's office, as his tonsils were cut from his throat without anesthetic. Several years later that doctor would be institutionalized in an insane asylum, and his gory efforts to extricate Cobb's tonsils were ample evidence to prove his madness. Schaefer, a good-natured German from Chicago, helped the recovering Cobb back to the hotel after the procedure.[8]

The Tigers finally arrived in Detroit on April 16, scheduled to kick off their 1906 season the following day against the White Sox. The Tigers had several new faces in 1906, including outfielder Davy Jones, a hyperactive character from Wisconsin who had played for the Cubs as recently as 1904, and then spent a season in the American Association where he hit .348 and showed great speed. Jones once joked: "Baseball wasn't a very respectable occupation back then. . . . I was going with a girl one time and after I became a professional ball player her parents refused to let her see me anymore."[9] Jones had won the center field job, beating out Cobb and Jimmy Barrett, to the delight of McIntyre and much of the rest of the team. A fresh face was also behind the plate in the person of Charles "Boss" Schmidt, a giant man with a sunny disposition who filled a void at that position. The remainder of the team filled out much as it had when Ty arrived at the end of 1905. Sam Crawford would be in right field, McIntyre in left, second baseman Schaefer and shortstop Charley O'Leary paired up the middle, Bill Coughlin was back at third, and Chris Lindsay was at first. The pitching staff once again revolved around George Mullin, Wild Bill Donovan, and Ed Killian, each of whom had won at least 18 games the previous season. For assistance, the Tigers had purchased Francis "Red" Donahue, a veteran right-hander with thirteen years of professional experience, from Cleveland.

Cobb had entered spring training hoping to land a starting job, but fine play by Jones and the distraction of his mother's trial kept him from that goal. As the season was set to begin, Cobb was the Tigers fourth outfielder, and there was no guarantee that he would get much playing time at all. Detroit, after their surprising late-season run in 1905, had hopes of contending with the better teams in the American League, Chicago and Philadelphia. In the first five years of the league's existence, Detroit had compiled a 332–379 record, which ranked a disappointing sixth in the league. After a third-place finish in the inaugural 1901 campaign, Detroit had slumped to seventh, fifth, and seventh, before rebounding to third in 1905. Bill Armour was the franchise's fifth manager in five-plus seasons, and fans in the city were hungry for some consistency and success.

In 1906, the city of Detroit was not yet the industrial behemoth that it would later become. Detroit was a city of roughly 300,000 people, making it the second smallest market in the major leagues, ahead of only Washington D.C. After the reshuffling of the American League in 1901 and 1902, when Milwaukee and Baltimore were moved to St. Louis and New York, respectively, there was speculation that the Detroit franchise might be shifted if attendance did not improve. In fact, Bancroft "Ban" Johnson, the president of the AL, debated in 1901 as to whether or not Detroit should be included in the AL landscape at all. As far as attendance, Detroit was a struggling franchise. In 1905 they had finished a distant last in league attendance, luring just 193,000 spectators to home games, a modest 2,545 per game. In each of the previous four seasons, the Tigers had finished no higher than sixth in attendance.[10]

The owner of the Detroit Tigers was William Hoover Yawkey, a 31-year-old playboy who inherited a logging and mining empire and quickly aimed his efforts at oil, where he made a small fortune, mostly in West Virginia. Yawkey was an opportunist with a sharp business mind who had bought the franchise from Samuel F. Angus in 1903. Yawkey spent much of his time in New York, where he ran his business interests and sailed on his many boats. Consequently, the Tigers were operated on a day-to-day basis largely by Frank J. Navin, the club secretary, who was actually a few years older than his boss. Navin, a former bookkeeper for an insurance agency, was a thrifty man with an eye on the bottom line. Subsequently, Detroit had one of baseball's lowest payrolls. Crawford, the biggest star on the team, was drawing little more than $2,500 per year, a figure far below that of other players of his stature.

But Navin and Yawkey were in the right place at the right time, and their fortunes, along with that of the ballclub, were about to change dramatically. The city of Detroit, which previously had relied chiefly on the lumber and iron ore industries, was in the midst of a transformation. By 1910, the city would have grown to almost 500,000 people, a rate of growth unequalled in such a short time in American history to that point.[11] Henry Ford's "horseless carriage" was the first product to be mass-produced for the public, and it invigorated the economy of the city, making it the industrial center of the nation. The demand for labor in the automotive plants would become so great that Ford Motor Company and their rival, General Motors, would pay to have workers move to Michigan. Those workers, when they had leisure time, would want to watch the national pastime, and the Tigers were the best show in town.

On April 17, the Tigers opened their 1906 season at Bennett Park in front of a franchise record crowd of nearly 14,000. Many fans stood behind roped off sections in the deep reaches of the outfield. Cobb watched the game from the bench, as Jones got the nod in center field. The Tigers disappointed their large crowd, losing 5–3 to Frank Owen and the White Sox, but they bounced back to win the next two games in the series. Ty saw his first action of the regular season on April 21, in Detroit's fifth game, when Crawford injured his leg. With Crawford sidelined for a week, Cobb continued to play in right field, though Armour still distrusted Cobb's ability in the clutch and frequently removed him for a pinch hitter. Yet, Cobb was resilient, and he hit the ball well enough against Cleveland in late April that when Crawford returned, Cobb was inserted in center field in place of the slumping Jones. Cobb responded to Armour's leap of faith by dazzling his opponents with his favorite weapon—the bunt. In the off-season Cobb had worked tirelessly to improve his bunting. He would spread out a sweater in front of the plate and practice for hours bunting the ball so it would come to rest on the sweater.[12] On May 17, Detroit was in Philadelphia for the second game of a four-game set with the Athletics. On the mound was the eccentric Rube Waddell, a hulking man-child with a durable left arm. Waddell was in his prime, having won twenty games for four consecutive seasons and four straight strikeout titles. Cobb, leading off the top of the first inning, dragged the first pitch from Waddell down the first base line for a perfect bunt single. Unfortunately for the Tigers, Cobb proved to be the only Detroit runner, as Rube set down the next twenty-seven batters in order for a one-hitter. Continuing to play on an everyday basis, Cobb was batting above .300 in mid-May, and his defensive play was spectacular as well. In Boston he saved a game when he made an over-the-shoulder grab, and twice in Washington he recorded assists on throws to third base.

In June, Cobb went on a tear that lifted his batting mark over .350, a figure near the league leader, Nap Lajoie of Cleveland. But later that month he began to slip, and soon he was in a slump that lowered his batting average by thirty points. At the same time, Cobb continued to have run-ins with a few of his teammates. McIntyre, always a nemesis, still despised Cobb, and refused to relay signals to his teammate when Ty was on base in front of him. When Cobb briefly took McIntyre's spot in left field, the veteran publicly embarrassed Cobb and attempted to turn Donovan and Schaefer, two of Ty's few friends on the club, against him.

The constant harassment from McIntyre and the others was too much for Cobb to bear. On July 18, with the team in Boston, Cobb was absent from the Detroit line-up, with newspaper accounts reporting that he was back in Detroit resting. Biographer Charles Alexander suggests that Cobb had "suffered some kind of emotional and physical collapse."[13] Whatever it was, Cobb missed several weeks of action, resting in Detroit. At some point he underwent surgery to remove an ulcer, and his condition improved after that. The ulcer was most likely brought on by the stress of his mothers' trial, his subsequent battle for a job in spring training, his tonsillitis, and the hazing he received from his teammates. For a 19-year-old away from home for an extended period for the first time in his life, the stresses on Cobb in 1906 were tremendous.

Eventually Cobb was strong enough to return, joining the team in St. Louis on September 3. Inserted in the fourth spot in the order, Cobb collected a single and swiped a base, but also made a miscue in the field that cost the Tigers the game. But Cobb's absence, combined with injuries to others (including a season-ending hernia to Davy Jones), had cost the Tigers. When he left the club on July 18, Detroit was 41–37, seven games back of the league-leading Athletics. When Cobb came back on the morning of September 3, they were four games under .500, fourteen and one-half games back of the "Hitless Wonders" White Sox. The Tigers had struggled to a 15–23 record without their 19-year-old center fielder. Cobb's return ignited the Detroit offense, and before long he was back to his old tricks on the basepaths. Against the Senators, Cobb went from first to third base on a sacrifice bunt, and in a contest against the White Sox in South Side Park, he scored from third on a pop-up to the shortstop. One newspaper glowed: "Cobb has been only two years in big league baseball, but is hailed as one of the greatest players the game has ever developed. He is a hard hitter, sure fielder and the greatest base runner baseball has ever seen."[14]

At the tail end of the season, Cobb was confident that he belonged in the big leagues, and he let his brashness between the white lines show. In two games against the A's, with catcher Ossee Schreckengost behind the plate, Cobb swiped four bases, including third and home. On October 1, in Cleveland against the Naps, Cobb belted his second career home run, a shot off Bob Rhoads. Unlike his lone homer the previous season, this home run went out of the park.

But the season did not finish without controversy. On October 6, in St. Louis against the Browns, Cobb and McIntyre clashed once again. George Stone, the Browns' left fielder and soon-to-be AL batting champion, lined a single to left center. Cobb and McIntyre converged but neither made a play for the ball as it rolled to the outer regions and Stone circled for a two-run homer. The pair of runs proved pivotal, as St. Louis defeated Detroit 4–2. After winning ten of eleven games, the Tigers had now dropped four straight. Armour and most of his players were on edge. Pitcher Ed Siever, who was tagged with the loss on the misplay by Cobb and McIntyre, was enraged. On the bench after the play, Siever blamed Cobb, shouting at the Georgian in front of the team and fans seated nearby. Cobb challenged Siever to fight him right there. Cooler heads prevailed, but after the game, in the clubhouse, Siever and Cobb crossed paths again, with teammates stepping in to curtail a fight. Later, in the team hotel, Siever verbally assaulted Cobb, but the younger player simply walked away from the confrontation. Finally, after Siever returned to curse Cobb and took a swing at him, Ty had endured enough. Cobb dodged the punch and delivered a blow of his own, sending Siever, who was 5 feet, 11 inches and 190 pounds, hurtling to the floor. As Siever lay sprawled, Cobb attacked him viciously, punching and kicking him in the head and arms. Later, Cobb recalled: "I was forced into a fight with Eddie Siever, a pitcher, in the Planter's Hotel lobby in St. Louis. He abused me for losing a ball game and said things that no man could stand for. I licked him and I licked him thoroughly."[15]

The following afternoon in Chicago, the Tigers finished their season, defeating the White Sox 6–1, behind Ed Killian. But the season as a whole had been bitterly disappointing for Detroit. The team slumped to sixth place with a 71–78 record, twenty-one games out of first place. More importantly to Navin, just 174,000 fans had come to see them play in Bennett Park, a 10 percent decrease from the previous year. Only Washington drew fewer spectators.

Cobb finished the year with a .320 batting average in 98 games, 112 hits, 45 runs scored, 13 doubles, 7 triples, a home run, and 34 RBIs. He stole 23 bases, and his .355 on-base percentage was the best on the team. In just his second season in the majors, which was technically his rookie campaign, Cobb's batting average ranked fourth in the league. Despite his fine showing and his emergence as one of the best players in the league, Cobb was not happy with the abuse he'd endured during the 1906 season. "I'd dreamed of becoming part of the Detroit organization, and all I'd known, so far, was jealousy and persecution."[16]

NOTES

1. Richard Bak, *Ty Cobb*, 16.
2. Caleb Chitwood letter, National Baseball Hall of Fame Library.

3. Bak, *Ty Cobb*, 17.

4. E. A. Batchelor, *Detroit Free Press*, August 30, 1905, 9.

5. Bill Armour file, National Baseball Hall of Fame Library.

6. Charles C. Alexander, *Ty Cobb*, 38.

7. Sam Crawford file, National Baseball Hall of Fame Library.

8. Alexander, *Ty Cobb*, 41.

9. Davy Jones file, National Baseball Hall of Fame Library.

10. Sean Forman, www.baseball-reference.com.

11. U.S. Census Bureau, *Population Statistics and Urban Growth, 1876–1919* (Washington, DC: U.S. Federal Government, 1991), 4–47.

12. Alexander, *Ty Cobb*, 90.

13. Ibid., 45.

14. *Chicago Ledger*, September 15, 1906, 10.

15. Cobb, with Stump, *My Life in Baseball*, 67.

16. Ibid., 26.

CHAMPIONS OF THE AMERICAN LEAGUE

Following the tragic death of his father in 1905, and his difficult 1906 season as a rookie with the Tigers, Ty Cobb was nervous entering spring training in Augusta, Georgia, in March of 1907. Despite his fine performance at the plate in 1906, Cobb was unsure if he could stomach another season of conflict with his own teammates. His contract for the season called for a raise to $2,400, only a few hundred dollars less than Frank Navin was paying Sam Crawford, who had eight years of experience in the big leagues and owned a career .300 average.

Samuel Earl Crawford hailed from Wahoo, Nebraska, earning himself the nickname "Wahoo Sam." After a brief career as a barber, at the age of 19, Crawford garnered his first look in the big leagues, playing for the Cincinnati Reds of the National League in 1899. Playing in Cincinnati's League Park, he belted 16 homers to lead the NL in 1901, but when he received little compensation for his efforts, he jumped to the Tigers prior to the 1903 campaign. By then he had already established his trademark of belting three-base hits. By the time he would hang up his spikes he would own the major league record for triples with an astonishing 312.[1] Throughout their years together in Detroit, Crawford and Cobb maintained a cordial alliance, and with the two of them usually batting back-to-back in the line-up, they established an unspoken form of communication, which helped them frequently perform double steals and trick plays. Crawford would later boast that he and Cobb were masters at frustrating opponents with their base-running antics: "Sometimes they'd get us, but usually they wouldn't."[2]

This is a posed stationary action shot of Cobb sliding into third base. © *Bettmann/CORBIS.*

Shortly after arriving in Augusta, Cobb found an ally in new Detroit manager Hughie Jennings, who had been hired to replace Bill Armour. Jennings had enjoyed a very successful career as shortstop for the famous Baltimore Orioles of the National League in the 1890s. Under the tutelage of baseball legend Ned Hanlon, Jennings teamed with John McGraw, Wilbert Robinson, Wee Willie Keeler, and Joe Kelley to form baseball's greatest team from 1894 to 1898. The Orioles won three straight pennants and twice finished second during that era, but it was the way that they won that caught attention. With Jennings, McGraw, Keeler, and Kelley leading the way, the Orioles used the hit-and-run, sacrifice bunt, suicide squeeze play—and several other plays of questionable legality—to frustrate and confuse their opponents. Jennings favorite ploy was to grab the belt of opposing runners as they tagged up on second base ready to head for third. He was also known to toss pebbles to the right of runners as they crept off the bag, wait for them to turn their heads, and sneak behind them for the throw from the pitcher. Ending his full-time playing career with Brooklyn in 1903, Jennings managed in the Eastern League for a few seasons before the Tigers bought his contract and named him their manager for the 1907 season. Like old teammates McGraw and Robinson, Jennings would soon find success as a skipper.

Frank Navin had hired Jennings to spite American League President Ban Johnson, who had declared an unofficial ban on colorful managers in his league. The National League had on occasion received bad publicity from the controversial managers in their circuit, and Johnson wanted to avoid the same situation. But Navin ignored Johnson's edict in the winter of 1906 and hired Jennings, a fiery manager with a strong personality. Navin's motivation for the insubordination came from the fact that the Tigers were being outdrawn at the gate by nearly every club in the league. With Jennings on the sidelines, Navin hoped to spark an interest.

Jennings took Cobb aside early in the spring of 1907, giving his outfielder advice on how to deal with his teammates and his own temper. Jennings also recognized that Cobb was a stubborn young man with great pride, and so he refused to give Cobb any playing tips. He preferred that Cobb figure out the game of baseball as he went along, knowing that Ty's talent would shine through. Jennings was skillful at dealing with Cobb almost from the beginning, relying on his experience as a lawyer. Jennings had been admitted to the bar of two states and practiced law in the off-season in Scranton, Pennsylvania.

Yet almost as quickly as Cobb had arrived and been taken under Jennings' wing, an incident occurred that nearly sent Ty packing. Less than a week into the training session, Cobb got into a scuffle with a black groundskeeper. The details of how the conflict started are in dispute, but there's no question that

Cobb slapped the groundskeeper, and later choked the man's wife when she intervened. Boss Schmidt, the Tigers catcher and the largest man on the team, responded by challenging Cobb to a fight, and after the rest of the team gathered around, including an incensed Jennings, the barrel-chested Schmidt pounded Cobb with blows to his head before the row was broken up.

Faced with the possibility of Cobb's unpredictable temper, and the growing faction of Cobb-haters in the Tigers clubhouse, Jennings decided he had to make a move. The evening of the incident, Jennings offered Cobb to Cleveland in a straight-up trade for outfielder Elmer Flick, a former batting champion. Flick was causing problems of his own, refusing to sign his contract with Cleveland and quarreling with manager Nap Lajoie. After mulling the offer for a brief time, Lajoie refused to trade Flick, and Cobb stayed with the Tigers. A few days later, Flick ended his holdout, but the trade that almost sent Cobb to Cleveland would haunt that team for years.

As the spring progressed, Cobb grew more isolated from his teammates. Much of it was Cobb's own fault, and the fight with Schmidt, who was popular with his teammates, didn't help matters. Cobb remained aloof and distant from his teammates and Jennings, speaking to his manager only when he requested a trade. Jennings tried to oblige, but a deal with the Highlanders fell through. Calls to other clubs drew the same response: they didn't want a troublemaker like Cobb on their team, or they were unwilling to offer value for the young outfielder. Jennings refused to part with Cobb unless he received talent in return, so he was stuck with the temperamental Georgian. Later, after he attempted to mend the relationship between Ty and his teammates, Jennings proclaimed, "Cobb is too good a hitter to let get away, when a little diplomacy will get the boys together."[3]

Later in the spring, just before the team was set to travel north for the start of the 1907 season, Cobb received permission to retrieve his mother and sister and have them accompany him to Detroit. Desiring the company of allies, and finding none in his own clubhouse, Cobb had his mother and sister stay with him in Detroit during the entire 1907 season. But their presence did not stop Cobb from squaring off with teammates. Late in the spring, Cobb and Schmidt fought again, this time under the stands before an exhibition game in Meridian, Georgia. Once again, the stronger Schmidt got the best of the action, with Ty suffering a broken nose and two black eyes. The fight only served to widen the valley between Cobb and the rest of the club. Interestingly, despite Cobb and Schmidt's repeated bouts, Schmidt was fair enough to recognize Ty's talent on the diamond, saying years later that he was "individually the greatest ball player who ever stepped on the field."[4]

In 1907, the Tigers were at a critical stage in franchise history. With their attendance having dropped in 1906, and after suffering an embarrassing sixth-place finish, Frank Navin was hopeful that Jennings could turn the ship around. Cobb would certainly be a large part of the puzzle, and if he could stay away from trouble with his teammates, Navin felt they had one of baseball's brightest talents. Still just 20 years old, the young Georgian had a bright future in the game. As far as the rest of the roster, Navin returned most of his regular ballplayers, with the lone exception of starting first sacker Chris Lindsay, who was replaced by Claude Rossman. A fine left-handed hitter, Rossman would be counted on to improve the production from that position. The other wrinkle on the team was at second base, where Germany Schaefer was unable to withstand a challenge from a rookie from Louisiana, Jerome "Red" Downs. Detroit would begin the season with a fresh right side of the infield. The outfield would also have an altered appearance. Bowing to pressure from Matty McIntyre, who still refused to play alongside Cobb, Jennings switched the versatile Crawford to center and placed Ty in right field, thus creating a buffer between the two enemies. The odd man out was Davy Jones, who would have to start the year riding the pine.

Detroit opened their regular season against Cleveland on April 11, earning a 2–0 victory behind the strong pitching of ace George Mullin. After a brief stretch of inconsistency, the team strung together a winning streak of five games, capped by a 13–5 pounding of the Browns on April 27. At 8–4, the team was tied for first place—a position they would haunt the entire season. Then in early May, McIntyre broke his ankle sliding into second base, opening the door for Jones to play regularly and lifting some psychological burden from Cobb. At the close of May, the Tigers were four and one-half games back of the defending league champion White Sox. In June, Jennings' squad hit a lull, going 12–12, but they were still within striking distance of the Sox at six and one-half paces back. Cobb was enjoying a stellar season, leading the league in batting as his average hovered around the .350 mark. On June 29, at home against Cleveland, Cobb stole home for the first of a record fifty-five times in his career, victimizing the battery of Heinie Berger and Howard Wakefield. On July 5, he did the same against Rube Waddell of the A's in a 9–5 Tiger triumph that launched the Tigers into a first place deadlock with the Philadelphia Athletics.

On August 2, Cobb faced Walter Johnson in the Washington pitcher's first big-league game. Johnson was a tall, long-armed pitcher from Kansas, who had been making headlines for his stellar pitching in leagues in California and Idaho. In his last stop, Johnson had struck out an amazing 166 batters in just 11 games, while hurling 75 consecutive shutout innings. In the second game of a double-header against the Tigers in Washington's American League Park, Johnson made his much anticipated major league debut. Prior to the contest, the Tigers did their best to rattle Johnson. Years later, Cobb said: "He was only a rookie, and we licked our lips as we warmed up. . . . We began to ride him as the game opened."[5] Several of the Tigers imitated a cow and mooed at Johnson, and others jeered the right-hander and called him "hayseed" as he strolled to the mound for the top of the first inning. But Johnson, whom Cobb would later select as the greatest pitcher of all-time, refused to be rattled, setting down the Tigers in order in the opening frame. In the second inning, Cobb led off against Johnson, and quickly determined the best tactic for getting the best of the rookie. With Davy Jones having told Cobb that Johnson's fastball was the best he'd ever seen, Ty wasted little time in bunting Johnson's offering to first base, beating out a hit. Seeing that Ty's strategy had caught Johnson unaware, Rossman followed with a similar drag bunt, easily beating it out for another single. On the play, Cobb kept running around second base, charged into third, and slid in safely with a perfect fade-away slide. When Downs followed with a fly ball, Cobb tagged and scored the first run ever allowed in the big leagues by Johnson. Cobb and Johnson would battle each other for twenty-one seasons in the American League, with Ty insisting "his fastball looked about the size of a watermelon seed and it hissed at you as it passed."[6]

In addition to Cobb, Crawford was having a fine season, ranking second to Cobb in the batting ranks. Rossman, the new first baseman, was also enjoying a great year, and his bunting skills were especially helpful batting directly behind Cobb, who was often on base agitating enemy pitchers. At the top of the order, the singles-hitting Jones was on his way to a .273 year and 101 runs scored. Cobb's pal, Germany Schaefer, had reclaimed the second base job from Red Downs, and was enjoying his finest year at the big league level. The Detroit offense quickly earned a reputation throughout the league. The *Washington Star* called it "an aggregation of the most aggressive players now playing ball."[7]

On the mound, Ed Killian—nicknamed "Twilight Ed" because of his penchant for pitching long games—was on his way to 25 wins. Backed by the potent Tiger offense, Bill Donovan was having a banner year as well, on his way to a 25–4 record and a 2.19 ERA. Mullin was his usual reliable self, and Siever had recovered from a poor spring training to pitch effectively. Behind their workhorse four-man staff and an offense that would score almost 100 runs more than any other team in the AL, Detroit entered September in the middle of the franchise's first pennant race. Their rivals for league supremacy were the Philadelphia Athletics, managed by Connie Mack, who also was the team owner. Mack was 44 years old, and in the seventh year of what would be a fifty-year reign over the A's. His team was built on pitching and defense. His staff included three future Hall of Fame pitchers: "Gettysburg Eddie" Plank, Charles "Chief" Bender, and the zany Rube Waddell, who was on his way to his sixth consecutive strikeout title. Ossee Schreckengost, one of baseball's best defensive catchers, was behind the plate to thwart the running game. Veterans Harry Davis and Jimmy Collins were at the corners, and outfielders Ralph "Socks" Seybold, Reuben "Rube" Oldring, and Tully "Topsy" Hartsel provided punch. Mack had guided essentially the same group to the pennant in 1905, and experts gave him the nod to win the battle in 1907 against Detroit. Complicating matters were the White Sox and Naps, who were just 2½ and 3½ games back of the frontrunners as September began.

The Tigers began September playing inconsistently, and fell behind Mack's A's by a single game. After playing .500 ball for another week, Detroit found themselves three games behind Philadelphia as they opened a four-game series against the White Sox at Bennett Park. By this time, Navin had installed temporary seating behind center field, increasing the park's capacity. Detroit won the first two games against Chicago 7–0 and 9–1, as Cobb collected four hits, drove in three, scored three runs, and swiped two bases in the second game he scored from first base on a long single. In New York, Detroit snatched two of three from the Highlanders, and then swept Boston to move a half-game in front. On September 27, the Tigers and A's opened a pivotal three-game series in Philadelphia. With a little over a week left in the season, the clash would factor heavily in the outcome of the pennant race.

Columbia Park, the site of the series, was one of the largest parks in the league, holding a normal capacity crowd of about 14,000. Located in the Brewerytown section of Philadelphia at the corner of Columbia Avenue and 29th Street, it had been host to every game ever played by the Athletics in the American League. On Friday, September 27, the Tigers sent Wild Bill Donovan out to face Eddie Plank. The two teams battled back and forth, but a late miscue by the A's defense handed the game to the Tigers 5–4. Detroit now held a one and one-half game lead in the race. The next afternoon's game was cancelled due to rain, and because it was illegal to play baseball in Philadelphia (or, for that matter, *anywhere* in the state of Pennsylvania) on Sunday, the three-game set would have to be finished on Monday with a double-header.

Given the extra rest, Donovan returned to the mound for Detroit, while Mack countered with his spit ball artist, "Sunny Jim" Dygart. It would prove to be an epic struggle, which Cobb later described as his greatest game. Donovan had little to offer early on and was shelled for seven runs in six innings, as the A's delighted an overflow crowd of more than 24,000 by building a 7–1 lead. Dygert was unable to last through the second inning however, and Mack replaced him with his ace Waddell. But in the visitor's half of the seventh inning, the Detroit bats came to life against the left-handed fastballer. The big blow in the four-run inning was a two-run double by Crawford, which made the score 7–5. The two teams then exchanged runs in the next frame to make it 8–6 entering the ninth inning. Crawford started the top of the Tigers ninth by singling to right field. Then Ty strolled to the plate to face Waddell. Cobb, having fared poorly against left-handed pitching his first two seasons in the big leagues, had worked hard to improve that deficiency. After watching a fastball go past for a strike, Cobb swung at Waddell's second offering, a curveball. The ball soared beyond the stunned overflow crowd in right field for a home run, tying the game in dramatic fashion. It was the biggest hit of Cobb's young career. The blow caused the normally stoic Mack to fall off the A's bench in disbelief. It was the end for Waddell, who was removed for Friday's starter Plank. Donovan, still in the game despite his early failures, responded to Cobb's blast by rearing back to shut down the A's in the bottom of the ninth, sending the game into extra innings.

For the 24,000 fans on hand at Columbia Park and the thousands more listening to reports back in Detroit, the drama was both exciting and nerve wracking. In the top of the tenth inning, Detroit struck for a single run, but Philadelphia tallied a run of their own in the bottom of the inning to extend the game farther. Plank and Donovan pitched unscathed over the next three innings. Then, in the bottom of the fourteenth, Harry Davis, the A's slugging first baseman, lofted a deep fly to center field over Crawford's head. Wahoo Sam felt his way back to the roped-off section where the playing field met the throngs of spectators (this was years before the advent of warning tracks) and settled under the ball. But before he could catch it, two policemen working crowd control bumped into Crawford, causing him to drop the ball. The Tigers cried foul as an argument erupted between Jennings, Crawford, and the two umpires on duty, Silk O'Laughlin and Tom Connolly. After Connolly made the ruling that Davis was out on fan interference, the A's dugout exploded in protest. Waddell, by this time in street clothes after Cobb's homer had knocked him from the ballgame, was enraged. After a scuffle, Donovan, Tiger first baseman Claude Rossman, and Waddell were removed from the game. At the same time, Cobb and the several other Tiger players were surrounded by the enraged crowd, who had spilled onto the field from behind the ropes in the outfield.

Eventually order was restored and the game was resumed. When Donovan surrendered a single to Danny Murphy, the crowd was once again riled, realizing that the umpire's decision had cost their team a run. But Donovan got out of the inning and Plank continued to stymie the Tigers. After seventeen innings, with darkness swallowing the ballpark, the umpires called the game with the score tied 9–9. The second game of the double-header was cancelled, and Detroit left Philadelphia with a one and one-half game lead. The controversy over Connolly's interference ruling raged on after the game. It didn't help matters that A's outfielder Topsy Hartsel overheard home plate umpire O'Laughlin disagree with Connolly's ruling. "What are they arguing about?" O'Laughlin reportedly said, "I saw no interference." Later, Mack gathered testimony from eyewitnesses and from the two policemen who had collided with Crawford. Their sworn affidavits were sent to league president Ban Johnson, but the decision on the field remained final. For years, Mack refused to speak to O'Laughlin, whom he felt had failed in overruling Connolly.[8]

The Tigers traveled to Washington the next day to play the Senators, whom they swept in four straight games, thanks to the incredible hitting of Cobb. In 18 at-bats in the 4 games, Cobb collected 13 hits, stole 5 bases, and scored 7 runs. The Tigers lead was now too large for Philadelphia to overcome. On October 5, in Sportsman's Park in St. Louis, where almost exactly a year earlier Cobb and teammate Ed Siever had been involved in their bloody fight, the Tigers clinched their first American League pennant. Ironically, it was Siever who was the benefit of a 10–2 victory, which included a triple and a home run by Cobb.

Cobb had won his first batting title, hitting .350 with 212 hits, also a league-leading total. He had played in nearly every game of the season, scoring 97 runs, with 29 doubles, 15 triples, 5 home runs (second to Harry Davis), and 116 RBIs. Cobb also led the league with 49 stolen bases, nearly a quarter of them coming in the last few weeks of the season. His performance led the Tigers to a .266 team batting average, a figure that was twelve points higher than the next closest team mark.

Though he had once struggled to hit left-handed pitching, Cobb became proficient at it in 1907, thanks in part to his off-season batting practice against southpaw and fellow Georgian, Nap Rucker.[9] Cobb had even solved the puzzle of White Sox lefty Guy "Doc" White, who had given Ty fits the first few times they had faced off. Crawford, hitting in front of Cobb, had also enjoyed a fine campaign: batting .323 with 102 runs scored, and 17 of his trademark triples. Jones had been valuable in the leadoff spot, and the additions of Rossman and Schmidt had solidified the first base and catching positions.

The Tigers had improved by twenty-one games, recording a 92–58 record. Within days, the celebration of Detroit's first AL flag was replaced by preparations for the World Series against the Chicago Cubs, champions of the National League. The Cubs were a juggernaut, having easily won their second straight pennant with 107 victories. The team, led by first baseman-manager Frank Chance, was anxious to avenge their embarrassing 1906 World Series loss to the White Sox. With that determination, they headed into their match against the Tigers.

On October 8, two days after their AL schedule had ended, Detroit traveled to Chicago to meet the Cubs at West Side Park. With a World Series–record crowd in attendance, Detroit took a 3–1 advantage into the bottom of the ninth behind Donovan's pitching. But when Schmidt allowed a passed ball on strike three to Del Howard, the Cubs had the makings of a rally, eventually tying the game 3–3. Subsequently, the two teams battled for twelve innings before darkness forced the game to be stopped, the first World Series game after the turn of the century to end in a tie. Cobb went 0 for 4 with a sacrifice bunt and a walk. The highlight of his day came prior to the game, when he was presented with a diamond-studded medal in honor of his batting championship.

The next day, the Tigers squandered an early 1–0 lead and eventually lost to Jack Pfiester and the Cubs 3–1. Cobb managed only a single in the loss. The series trend was already developing: the Cubs were running wild against the Tigers. By the end of the series Chicago would have 18 stolen bases to their credit, as Jennings desperately tried to stop the attack by playing four different men behind the plate.

With Cobb singling once, Siever lost Game 3, 5–1, and the two teams headed to Detroit. On October 11, Detroit hosted their first World Series game, but once again Chicago ran wild, winning 6–1 over Donovan, as Ty scored the only Tiger run following a triple. George Mullin tried to keep the Series alive the next afternoon, but in front of a disappointing crowd of 7,369 at Bennett Park, the Tigers were whitewashed 2–0 by Mordecai "Three Finger" Brown. Cobb doubled in the finale, but his overall performance in the Series was unspectacular. He had hit .200 (4 for 20) with no stolen bases. The Tigers had been limited to a paltry .209 average by the Cub pitching staff.

Despite the loss in the World Series, it had been a successful season for the Detroit Tigers, one that left both Yawkey and Navin very pleased. The players were pleased as well, when each member of the club earned $1,946 in World Series money. For many of the players, it was more than they had earned all year in salary. In addition, team attendance had improved by more than 1,200 per game in 1907. With a successful, exciting young team, and with their 20-year old batting champion, the Tigers had a bright future.

After the World Series ended, Cobb played in a series of exhibition games against the Cubs in Chicago, which netted him some more money. Then Ty returned to Royston for the off-season. With his financial success, Cobb was able to pay off much of the family debt and had funds left over to make improvements to the farm. He again spent much of his time hunting and working on the farm, though he did carve out time to court the young Charlotte Lombard, daughter of the prominent Roswell Lombard family in Augusta.

In January, Cobb received his contract from Navin for the 1908 season, which called for $3,000. The figure offended Cobb, who, having just become the youngest player to ever win a batting title, knew he was a valuable ballplayer. Ty sent the contract back to Detroit unsigned and began the first of many salary battles in his career. Cobb wanted a few assurances heading into his third full season in the big leagues. He wanted to be excluded from the rule that stated a club could release a player with just ten days notice, and more importantly, he wanted Navin to give him $5,000 a year for three years. The demand was quite a shock to Navin, who expected loyalty and respect from his players. The fact that a 21-year-old ballplayer—batting champion or not—was dictating such bold financial terms was unacceptable.

Navin was bargaining from a position of power. Baseball players in the early 1900s were little more than slaves to the owners; they were pieces of property that were bought, sold, and released without a second thought. Very few players were given more than a one-year contract, which meant that uncertainty was a constant companion to the early-twentieth-century ballplayer. Players who wanted more money had very few options if clubs refused accept their demands. If a player was to hold out, he may be blackballed from the big leagues and be forced to find employment in another field of work or latch on with one of the "rebel" or "outlaw" leagues, which worked outside the confines of Organized Baseball.

Within days, Ty's holdout was the biggest news in baseball, with Cobb receiving little support in the newspapers. Sportswriters, who made little money themselves and were often treated poorly by players, rarely defended the ballplayers in salary disputes. But the owners were making far more money than they were doling out to their pawns on the field. And though a labor union for ballplayers was decades away, the treatment of professional players was enough to cause many stars to hold out, sometimes for a full season. In the early 1900s, it was not uncommon for players to jump leagues in midseason for better pay elsewhere. A good ballplayer could turn the tables on the owners and turn the system upside down to get the money he deserved. Cobb felt he was worthy of a top salary. When Navin informed Cobb that Crawford, a veteran of many seasons, had signed for $4,000, Cobb was undaunted. He continued to demand a multiyear deal worth $5,000 annually.

In March, Cobb accepted Navin's invitation to come to Detroit for face-to-face negotiations. After two long sessions, Cobb agreed to accept a one-year deal and drop his demand of exemption from the ten-day release clause. But he still insisted on a higher salary than Crawford. Finally, Navin agreed to pay Cobb $4,000 for the year with an option for a $800 bonus if Ty hit .300 again. Cobb was satisfied with the potential $4,800 earnings, which was just $200 less than what he wanted. Grudgingly, he would have to wait for another time to get a multiyear deal, which was something he felt he needed to insure his future. He was determined to get as much out of baseball as he could.

After a quick trip back to Royston, Ty traveled to Little Rock, Arkansas, where the Tigers were training for the first time. Helped by his off-season regiment of hunting, Cobb's was in excellent condition. Despite a short bout with the flu, Ty was well prepared to defend his batting title, and was in the line-up on April 14 in Chicago's West Side Park when the 1908 campaign began. Picking up where he left off in the stretch drive the previous year, Cobb collected three hits, including a long home run to right field, but Detroit lost their opener. Three days later they lost their home opener as well, with Ty's mother and sister in the stands watching. The two would once again spend the regular season living with Ty in his apartment not far from Bennett Park. In April, the Tigers struggled to a 3–9 record as their offense sputtered. But Cobb did his part to win: in the first few weeks of the season he was hitting over .360 and creating havoc on the basepaths.

The 1908 Tigers returned nearly every member of the previous season's AL champion club. Unfortunately for Cobb, McIntyre was back in left field in place of Jones, but besides that, the other seven regulars were the same. Crawford, at 28, was entering his prime, and the rest of the team was fairly young. The pitching staff had added two more Ed's—Summers and Willett—to go along with Ed Killian and Ed Siever, while George Mullin and Wild Bill Donovan also returned to form a solid pitching corps. Languishing in last place, the Tigers emerged from their slumber on May 9 in the second game of a double-header, winning 5–2. That began a six-game winning streak, and a stretch of fourteen wins in eighteen games. On May 26, Detroit defeated the A's 1–0 behind Mullin, in their first clash with Philadelphia since the heated 1907 pennant race.

In June, Cobb's batting took a back seat to controversy. As he was leaving the Hotel Ponchartrain in Detroit one early June morning, Cobb inadvertently stepped on some asphalt that had just been laid by street workers. One of the men in the work party, a black man named Fred Collins, chastised Cobb for the mistake. Cobb responded by hurling Collins to the ground. Within a few days, after Collins realized who Cobb was, he pressed charges and threatened a lawsuit. The entire situation embarrassed Navin and the club. Finally, Cobb agreed to settle with Collins and avoid a trial. The *Detroit Free Press* reported in a June 22, 1908, article:

> It cost Tyrus Cobb, the American League's premier batsman, just $75 for his fracas with a negro by the name of Collins, an asphalt worker, who showed badly warped features for a week or more as a result of the street fight. Cobb, through his attorney, settled the matter out of court Saturday morning. "I settled only because I did not want to be inconvenienced later on," said Cobb. "I would act again in a similar manner under the same conditions. When a man is insulted it is

worth $75 to get satisfaction." Cobb's friends are greatly pleased over the outcome of the affair. The case might have dragged through the courts, as Cobb was determined to fight it out, regardless of cost.[10]

The fight with Collins was one of many racial incidents that Cobb instigated during his life. Like other southerners reared in the 1890s and early 1900s, Cobb carried definite prejudices. As a young man growing up in rural Georgia, most of the blacks Cobb came in contact with were laborers employed by his father on the family farm. There was a definite hierarchy in the relationship between the races. Blacks were expected to be respectful and submissive. They were not afforded the same rights as white people in the south. Blacks could not vote, nor attend white schools. Blacks in the south were very much segregated, both socially and politically. Violence against blacks was not uncommon in the years following the end of the Civil War, and they increased with the birth of the Ku Klux Klan, which was first established in Tennessee in 1866. Cobb grew up in that environment. Though it's unlikely that he ever joined the KKK, it's certain that he shared the bigoted views that many southerners believed. Throughout his life, Cobb clashed with blacks who failed to show the proper amount of "humility" in the presence of a white man.

On Memorial Day in Detroit against the White Sox, the Tigers swept a double-header and moved into first place. But inconsistent play dropped them in the standings until early July, when they rode a six-game winning streak back into first. Later that month, with Cobb and Crawford pacing the offense, Detroit won nine in a row to stretch their lead to three games over the surprising Browns. On July 17, Cobb enjoyed the first five-hit game of his career, banging out two singles, two doubles, and a triple against the A's in a 21–2 thrashing of Philadelphia. But in August, Detroit, playing uninspired baseball, recorded an 11–13 mark, allowing the Browns, as well as several other teams, to stay in the race.

That month, Cobb made headlines when he left the team briefly to return to Georgia. The purpose of his trip was to marry Charlotte Lombard. The wedding was a bit of a surprise to manager Jennings and the team, seeing as Cobb told them he was leaving just two days before his train was to depart. It was not uncommon at that time for players to leave their teams for personal business, but the fact that Cobb was doing it during a tight pennant race did not endear him to Tiger management or the press. On August 4, he left for Georgia, where he married Charlotte—whom he affectionately called "Charlie"—at her father's mansion, the Oaks, on August 6 in Augusta. Approximately twenty-five guests were on hand for the ceremony, which was performed by a Baptist preacher.[11]

Charlotte Marion Lombard, the daughter of Roswell Lombard, a prominent and wealthy man in Augusta, was 17 years old when she married Ty Cobb. She was an attractive woman, with dark hair and features. Family members described her as "shy and dignified" and "warm and loving." She had beautiful brown eyes and a sturdy figure. Cobb and his new bride arrived in Detroit late on August 8, and Ty was back in uniform the next day to face Washington. In his first game as a married man, Cobb singled, stole a base, and tripled in a 5–2 Detroit victory.

In the middle of September, with three weeks left in the season, Detroit was in first place with a one and one-half game lead over the White Sox, with Cleveland trailing by two games, and St. Louis two and one-half back; Connie Mack's A's, expected to challenge the Tigers once again, were well behind in sixth place. On September 15, the Tigers were in St. Louis facing Jimmy McAleer's club, which featured Philadelphia exile Rube Waddell, who had escaped Mack's clutches. Behind the hard-throwing lefty and the hitting of outfielder George Stone, McAleer had kept his team in the hunt for the pennant. But when Detroit defeated the Browns 8–7 on the fifteenth, and then Waddell was beaten the next day, St. Louis was knocked from the race. Detroit then split four games with the Highlanders, while the White Sox and Naps continued to charge. Cleveland was in the middle of a nine-game winning streak, and would win sixteen of eighteen through September 23. Then, in Boston, the Tigers hit their low point of the season, suffering a three-game sweep at the hands of the mediocre Red Sox. The skid sent Detroit into third place, two and one-half games behind Nap Lajoie's red-hot Cleveland club. On September 25, Detroit played a double-header against the A's in Philadelphia and took the first game 7–2, as Cobb delivered three hits, including two doubles. On the bases he terrorized Ossee Schreckengost once more, stealing two. In the second game, Jennings surprised everyone by pitching Ed Summers, who had started and won the first game. Summers rose to the challenge, hurling a 1–0, ten-inning, two-hit victory. The rookie right-hander was taking his place alongside Mullin as the Tigers most reliable hurler. The double-header sweep moved the Tigers to within one-half game of first place Cleveland, who lost a heartbreaker to Washington when they gave up five runs in the ninth inning.[12]

The next two days saw two more wins for Cobb and the Tigers, as they completed a sweep of the Athletics. Washington came to town next, and the Tigers rolled to three more wins by a combined score of 18–9. That ended the month of September with Detroit on top, one-half game ahead of Cleveland, while Chicago lurked just one and one-half games behind. The Tigers had two games remaining at home against the Browns, and a three-game series with the White Sox in Chicago. Luckily for Detroit, Cleveland and Chicago would fight each other for two games starting October 2. That day, in Cleveland, with thousands of Naps fans roaring, ace Addie Joss handcuffed the White Sox 1–0 and pitched a perfect game. It was an amazing clutch performance in the middle of the three-way pennant race. Meanwhile, Detroit rallied with a pair of runs in the bottom of the ninth inning to win a thrilling game over St. Louis, 7–6. Cobb figured heavily in the win, scoring the final run after a bunt single. Earlier, he had collected a two-run single off Waddell in the first inning. The exciting win, in front of nearly 20,000 overflow spectators in Bennett Park, kept Detroit in first place. The next day, Donovan blanked the Browns 6–0, while the White Sox rebounded from Joss's perfection to win 3–2. The victory kept Chicago's faint pennant hopes alive. They were two and one-half games behind the Tigers with their three-game match set to start the next day. Cleveland was one and one-half games back, with four games left at St. Louis.

In their first game against the Sox, Detroit imploded. Three errors in the first inning let in three runs as the Tigers lost 3–1. White Sox owner Charles Comiskey bragged: "Chicago deserved to win. It's the greatest ball town in the world."[13] But the White Sox still needed to sweep the last two games against the Tigers to snatch the flag. In St. Louis, Cleveland played to a 3–3 tie, which left the three pennant-fighting teams just one and one-half games apart. But the following day, when Cleveland split a double-header and the White Sox defeated Summers and Detroit 6–1, the Naps were eliminated. Because of tie games (called due to darkness) that had never been replayed, the Naps would not have enough games to make up the difference. At that time, there was no league rule forcing teams to replay tie games.

The Tigers–White Sox finale of October 6, would decide the 1908 American League pennant race. The winner of the game would be league champion. Jennings did all he could to rally his team's spirits. After having won ten straight games to take charge of the race, their two losses to Chicago the previous two days had put their season in jeopardy. At the Lexington Hotel, Jennings gathered his team and gave them a fiery pep-talk prior to the bus ride to South Side Park. The team could have been forgiven if they were a little quiet that morning. The previous night, Chicago rooters had spent the evening outside the hotel shouting threats and catcalls at the team. Many of the Tigers, including Cobb, didn't fall asleep until four o'clock in the morning.

The pitching match-up featured Bill Donovan against Doc White. Both pitchers had won twenty games the year before, but had struggled in 1908. The Tigers jumped on White from the start. In the first, McIntyre singled and two batters later Crawford doubled him home. Ty came to the plate with the Chicago rooters jeering his every move. On the first offering from White, Cobb lined the ball into the left-center-field gap and slid into third with a run-scoring triple. That brought Ed Walsh into the game to relieve White, and after two more runs were plated, the Tigers had a comfortable 4–0 advantage. Donovan kept the White Sox at bay and cruised to a 7–0 victory and a second straight AL pennant. Cobb had rapped out three hits in the win, and once again, as at the end of the 1907 season, he proved to be valuable in the clutch. The victory was sweet for Cobb and his teammates: "We walloped them like they were sand-lotters," he said.[14]

Ty's final batting average was .324, which easily gave him his second straight batting crown. He also paced the league with 188 hits and 101 RBIs. Cobb had banged out 36 doubles, 20 triples, and 4 home runs. Once again, Crawford was second in the batting race, hitting .311, while McIntyre enjoyed his best season, hitting .295 with a league-high 105 runs scored. Rossman and Schmidt also provided batting support, as did rookie shortstop Donie Bush, who spent the first of fourteen seasons as Cobb's teammate.

The pitching staff had benefited from the addition of rookie Ed Summers, who won 24 games. Donovan's last-day win brought his total to 18, and Mullin (17 victories) and Willett (15) also proved steady. It was the deepest pitching staff the Tigers had ever had. Back at the Lexington Hotel in Chicago following their pennant-clinching win, the team honored Jennings with a shout of "Eee-yah ee-yah!"—his trademark rally cry from his third base coaching box. Jennings responded by telling his players that each of them would receive a brand new tuxedo, fulfilling a promise he and Navin had made during the spring. After a celebration dinner, in which several players became drunk on the overflowing champagne, the team boarded a train for Detroit. Upon their arrival early the next morning, they were greeted by nearly 1,000 fans, who cheered their heroes as they stepped off the train. A group of fans lifted Donovan onto their shoulders and carried him through the station, while the crowd sang, "Michigan, My Michigan." Later, the team rode in open cars to Detroit City Hall, where Cobb, Crawford, Donovan, and Jennings received the grandest reception.[15] Jennings told the gathered crowd that this time the Tigers would be ready for their National League foe in the World Series. That opponent was still unknown, because the Cubs and Giants were embroiled in a classic race for the pennant. The following day, the Cubs defeated the Giants in a one-game playoff for the National League crown, setting up a rematch of the previous season's World Series. Cobb and his teammates were anxious to redeem themselves and prove American League superiority.

The 1908 World Series opened in Detroit at Bennett Park. Hoping for a huge crowd, Navin had erected temporary bleachers around the outfield. Unfortunately, a steady drizzle kept thousands of fans home, and a disappointing crowd of 10,812 settled in to cheer their Tigers. Summers came on in relief of Killian in the fourth for Detroit and thanks to a few key hits by Cobb (three singles for two RBIs), he led 6–5 entering the top of the ninth. But, as they had the previous year, Detroit wilted in the final frame. The Cubs scored five runs, stunning the crowd and sending Detroit to a 10–6 defeat. Tiger bats had done their part, battering Ed Reulbach and Orval Overall, but when Three Finger Brown entered in the eighth inning they were stifled.

The next day the Series shifted to Chicago, where nearly 18,000 fans watched as Overall stymied Detroit on four hits, winning 6–1. Cobb did his part, singling in Detroit's lone run, but it was too little too late. In Game 3, Detroit's offense erupted for eight runs against Jack Pfiester and Reulbach, as George Mullin cruised to an 8–3 win. It was the Tigers first victory in a World Series game. Cobb was at his best, collecting four hits, including a double. He batted in a pair of runs and scored twice, but it was his daring base running that stood out. In the ninth inning, Cobb singled, and then stole second base on the first pitch. Prior to the next pitch he shouted to Reulbach that he was going to third, and did just that, beating a throw from Cubs catcher Johnny Kling. When Rossman followed with a walk, the Tigers tried to catch the Cubs off guard with one of their standard plays. Rossman trotted to first on the walk and then made a dash for second, drawing a throw. At the same instant, Cobb dashed for home. But the Cubs were wise and caught Cobb between home and third, with third baseman Steinfeldt applying the tag. Cobb had delighted the Chicago fans with his base running flair.

In Game 4, Brown was back on the mound for the Cubs. As a boy, Brown had suffered an injury on his family's farm that severed one of his fingers and part of another at the knuckle. The mishap proved to be a boon to his athletic career. As a pitcher, Brown's mangled hand had an exotic effect on the ball, causing it to dip and curve in a manner that fooled enemy batters. In 1908, he won 29 games, pitched 9 shutouts, and posted a dazzling 1.47 ERA in more than 300 innings of work. Against Detroit in Game 4, Brown allowed just four hits, striking out five and walking just one batter. Cobb was 0 for 4 and fanned once against the tough right-hander, who would one day join Cobb in the Hall of Fame. The Cubs now held a commanding three-games-to-one lead, and were poised to snatch their second straight title the next day back in Detroit.

Tiger bats continued their slumber in Game 5, as they managed just three hits against Overall, a tall right-hander from California. The Cubs pushed just two runs across against Summers, but that was enough to win the world championship, 2–0, in five games. Overall and Brown had combined to shackle the Tiger offense, winning all four games for the Cubs, behind their aggregate 0.61 ERA and 20 strikeouts in 29⅓ innings pitched. Cobb went 0 for 3 with a walk in Game 5, finishing with a team high .368 batting average (7 for 19) for the series. He led his team with 4 RBIs, 3 runs scored, 7 hits, and 2 steals. It was a great improvement over his miserable showing in the 1907 Series, but it was little comfort to him. Also of little comfort was the $871 Cobb and each of his teammates received for their World Series appearance. Unlike the previous year, when Yawkey had turned over the owner's share to the players, Navin kept his share. That decision, along with the small crowds at Bennett Park, left the players with a small bonus.

A few days after the Series ended, they had a chance to add to that figure when they traveled to Chicago and then Terre Haute, Indiana, to face the Cubs in a pair of exhibition games. Prior to the game in Chicago, Cobb was the lone Tiger participant in a series of skill events. The first required each player to drop a bunt in fair territory and run to first base. The fastest time would win. Cobb won that event, nipping Cubs' right fielder Frank "Wildfire" Schulte. In the next test, several Cubs and Cobb ran the 100-yard dash. Once again, Cobb and Schulte were the standouts, with Ty winning in a time of 10.25 seconds. Finally, players took turns rounding the bases, with Cobb's time of 13.75 seconds the fastest by nearly a full second. Cobb's performance won him the affection of the Chicago crowd, who had jeered him days earlier during the World Series.

Following the exhibitions, Cobb returned to Royston for the winter. But the winter of 1908–1909 would be busier than any he had enjoyed previously. In the few weeks following his arrival in Royston, Cobb took advantage of his growing celebrity and made several appearances around the country. In November, Cobb and his wife traveled to New Orleans where Ty spent nearly three weeks playing in a semipro league to earn extra money. They then returned to Royston, where Cobb received his contract for the 1909 season in January. Unlike the previous winter, Cobb signed his contract without incident, which called for a $5,000 base salary.

In March, Cobb went alone to San Antonio, Texas, for spring training. Over the winter, Ty had grown another inch, and now stood at a shade over 6 feet, 1 inch, weighing more than 180 pounds.[16] That would be Cobb's playing weight for the large portion of his prime years. At the conclusion of training, Charlotte met Ty, and the couple traveled together with the team north for the start of the season. On April 14 in Detroit, Cobb and the Tigers opened the 1909 season against the White Sox. Mullin shut down the Sox 2–0, as Ty pounded out a pair of hits. But the first month of the 1909 season, while it proved successful for the team as a whole, was tough for Cobb. While Cobb was hitting below .250, Detroit built a three-and-one-half-game lead in the American League.

The Tigers were once again built around their booming bats in the outfield and a workhorse pitching staff. Every one of the starters from 1908 had returned except third baseman Bill Coughlin, replaced by George Moriarty, who had been purchased from the Highlanders. Moriarty fit in nicely in the Detroit scheme: he was speedy and tough.

In June, Cobb lifted his average above the .300 mark, but he still trailed Eddie Collins of the Philadelphia A's by more than forty points in the batting race. As the two-time defending champion, Cobb was determined to make a run at Collins. During the season, newspapers took to calling him "The Georgia Peach," a nickname attributed to writer Grantland Rice. For most of the rest of his career, many of Cobb's friends would use "Peach" interchangeably with "Ty." In July, the Tigers won seventeen of thirty games, with Connie Mack's Athletics still on their tails. On August 6, Detroit opened a four-game set against the A's in Philadelphia with a 3–1 win behind Summers, who won his fifth straight game and boasted a 15–5 record. But the A's bounced back to take the next three games, battering Summers in the finale. Detroit and Philadelphia were deadlocked with identical 62–40 records. When the two rivals met later in August, Detroit was riding a five-game winning streak, but trailed the Athletics by a single game.

In the first meeting of their series, on August 24 at Bennett Park, Cobb played one of the most infamous games of his career. An incident took place in the first inning that would be remembered for decades. Cobb, batting third, drew a walk against Harry Krause, the Philadelphia lefty, then proceeded to swipe second base. When Crawford took ball four and trotted to first with a free pass, Cobb suddenly bolted for third base, taking catcher Paddy Livingstone by surprise. Livingstone heeded the screams of his teammates and fired the ball to third, where Frank Baker caught it and waited for Cobb, who seemed to be an easy out. But with all the time he had to await the charging Cobb, Baker inexplicably transferred the ball to his bare hand and reached over to tag the sliding runner. Ty's right foot reached back for the bag as he performed his patented fade-away slide. At that instant, Baker's arm and Cobb's spikes met, causing Baker to drop the ball and recoil in pain. As Baker held his arm, which was bleeding from a small cut, Cobb stood on third base defiantly as Mack argued that he should be called out for deliberately spiking Baker.[17] The A's lost the argument and Detroit won the game 7–6, as Cobb collected three hits. Later in the game, unshaken by the earlier controversy, Cobb stretched a long single into a double, sliding hard into Collins at second base, who ended up on his backside. Cobb collected two hits in each of the next two games, and the Tigers swept the fuming A's and opened up a two-game lead.

Uncharacteristically, Connie Mack responded to the Baker spiking with great emotion. The Philadelphia manager wrote a plea to Ban Johnson, asking that the AL president suspend Cobb for his dirty play. In response, Frank Navin sent a copy of the action photo of the play to the *Sporting Life*. Navin noted in his attached letter that "Mr. Johnson, President of our League, on seeing the picture, stated that Cobb was completely vindicated."[18] The photo showed that Cobb's slide was legitimate. The spiking, which was far from a dirty play, was not Cobb's fault. The incident caused a rift between the two teams, and later that season, when Cobb played in Philadelphia, he required police protection. Ty had received more than a dozen death threats from enraged Philadelphia fans, including one that promised to shoot him with a rifle from a window overlooking Shibe Park.

After the A's left Detroit, the Tigers proceeded to host New York, whom they pummeled 17–6 in the opener, as they continued their winning ways. On September 2, they finished their home stand having won fourteen straight games. During the streak they averaged 6.4 runs per game, a towering figure in the dead ball era. Cobb and Crawford, now batting in that order, provided much of the offense, batting a combined .423 during the skein. Ty had been a demon on the bases, stealing 10 bases in the fourteen games. With a month left in the season, Detroit led by five games, with Cobb a close second in the batting race to Collins, who was fading.

In Cleveland on September 3, after the stellar pitching of Summers and Addie Joss forced the Tigers and Naps into a tie game, Cobb was involved in an incident that was far more dangerous than the Baker spiking. Returning from a late dinner with a friend, Cobb arrived at the Hotel Euclid around 2:00 A.M. While entering the hotel elevator, Cobb became involved in a verbal argument with the elevator operator, a black man, whom he apparently slapped. Before he could get to his room, the security guard, also a black man, confronted Cobb, prompting the Georgian to beat the man with his own nightstick. The two men continued to fight, and at some point Cobb brandished a knife and made an attempt to slash the man, with the guard responding by pulling his pistol and hitting the ballplayer over the head. With both men having taken the fight to a dangerous level, witnesses intervened and separated the two. Cobb retreated to his room and emerged the following day with bruises on his face and a bandage on his head. Despite the injuries, Cobb played that day and collected three hits in the opener of a double-header, which Detroit lost.

After the games, as the team readied to leave for St. Louis, detectives went to League Park in search of Cobb, but he had already left. Within days, the security guard and the Hotel Euclid threatened lawsuits against Cobb and the Tigers, which prompted Navin to respond. The Tigers secretary used considerable guile and arm twisting to convince the hotel to drop the charges, and after a few days he was able to appease the security guard with a few hundred dollars and a promise to pay his medical bills. But the Cleveland Police Department refused to forget the incident, vowing to arrest Cobb the next time he showed up in the city.

Luckily for the Tigers, they were not scheduled to play in Cleveland the remainder of the year. However, there were issues between Cobb and the city of Philadelphia.

On September 15, the Tigers arrived in Philadelphia for a four-game series that would begin the next day, and would decide the pennant race. Still in a rage over the Baker spiking incident, a handful of Athletics' fans had written threatening letters to Cobb. One had promised Cobb that he would be "shot if he stepped on the field."[19] With potential danger as a backdrop, Detroit faced the A's on the sixteenth, with Cobb under heavy guard as he warmed up prior to the game. Eddie Plank then delighted the partisan crowd, which numbered more than 20,000, as he fanned Ty with the bases loaded in the fourth inning. Cobb went 0 for 4 as the Tigers lost 2–1. After the game, with his special guard detail off duty, Cobb ventured outside the team hotel for a walk and was surrounded by a crowd of angry Philadelphians. But with great courage and a sneer on his face, he walked through the crowd unharmed to get back to the safety of his hotel.[20] The next day, Detroit evened the score by beating the A's 5–3, as Cobb bunted safely twice and produced a run on a deep fly to right field. During the contest, he and Baker made amends, shaking hands at third base. The gesture seemed to help tame the crowd, who treated Cobb with less venom afterward. The Athletics won the last two games of the series, but still remained two games behind the Tigers with two weeks left in the season.

On September 29, with Detroit resting two and one-half games ahead of Mack's A's, Cobb's bat and Ed Killian's pitching arm sealed up the pennant. In a doubleheader at Huntington Avenue Grounds in Boston, Cobb went 5 for 7 with a walk, and Killian pitched two complete games, as Detroit clinched a tie for the pennant. The next day, when the White Sox swept the A's in a double-header, the Tigers had won their third straight American League flag. Cobb and several other regulars were sent back to Detroit, where they remained as the rest of the team finished the series in Boston and played two meaningless games against Chicago to wrap up the season. When the Tigers beat "Sleepy Bill" Burns on the final day of the season, they set a league record with their ninety-eighth win.

Cobb, whom the *Detroit Free Press* called "the most sensational young player who ever broke into the national game, and certainly the greatest ballplayer in the American League to-day,"[21] had won his third straight batting title. His batting average of .377 was more than thirty points higher the runner-up. The 22-year-old also paced the AL in runs (116), hits (216), home runs (nine), RBIs (107), stolen bases (76, which was a league record), and slugging (.517). He was unquestionably the best player in the league. Detroit sportswriter E. A. Batchelor wrote: "There never was a completely dull ball game if he was on the field."[22]

The Tigers had become the first American League team to win three straight pennants. They had done so on the shoulders of the league's most explosive offense, fueled by Cobb. Crawford once again was spectacular, hitting .314 with 97 RBIs. Switch-hitting shortstop Donie Bush, in his first full season, played in every game but one, and proved to be a wonderful leadoff man. He scored 114 runs, batted .273, stole 53 bases, and led the league in bases on balls. For the third straight season, Detroit led the American League in runs scored, and behind Cobb's daring thievery, they also topped the circuit in stolen bases with a total of 280.

In the World Series the Tigers faced the Pittsburgh Pirates, led by shortstop Honus Wagner, the best player in the National League. Every bit the match for Cobb, the 35-year old Wagner had also won the batting title. The press touted the match-up as a battle of the two finest players in the game. But the Pirates also featured Fred Clarke, a rangy right fielder with a shotgun arm, George Gibson, a fireplug catcher, and a formidable pitching staff. Howie Camnitz and Vic Willis gave the Pirates a pair of 20-game winners, and Albert "Lefty" Leifield had 19 wins to his credit. The Tigers were determined to avoid a third straight loss to the National League in the postseason.

As it turned out, it was not Camnitz (who missed most of the series due to a bout with tonsillitis), Willis, nor Leifield who the Tigers had to worry about. Rather, it was a little-known 27-year-old rookie with only thirty games of big league experience. In Game 1, played at Forbes Field in Pittsburgh, Charles "Babe" Adams defeated the Tigers 4–1, in the first of his three unlikely victories. Having pitched in twenty-five games that season for Pittsburgh, and a handful prior to 1909, Adams was little more than an afterthought to the aggressive Tiger hitters. But his slow delivery, which Pittsburgh manager Fred Clarke had been told resembled that of William "Dolly" Gray, a soft-tossing Washington hurler who had pitched well against Detroit earlier that year, frustrated the Tigers. Detroit's line-up preferred fastballs, and the bending curves and off-speed pitches that Adams showcased kept them off balance. Cobb scored the only Tiger run of the day in the first inning.

In Game 2, Detroit exacted some revenge, hitting Camnitz and Willis hard for a 7–2 win. In the third inning, Cobb shocked the Pittsburgh crowd when he stole home against Gibson. With the series knotted at one game each, Detroit fans came out in full force for Game 3, with 18,277 rooters at Bennett Park. But Ed Summers was rocked for five runs in the first inning and Detroit was in a 6–0 hole after two frames. Then Cobb helped them get back into the game with a run-scoring single in the seventh, as the home team plated four runs. But seldom-used reliever Ralph Works yielded two runs to the Pirates in the top of the ninth, and Detroit's two-run rally in the bottom of that inning was too little. Pittsburgh had won the game 8–6. The next day, Mullin won 5–0 on a chilly fall day in Michigan to tie the Series at two games apiece, as Cobb's double drove in two runs.

In Game 5, back in Pittsburgh, Adams twirled his magic again, winning 8–4 despite three hits by Crawford and a single by Cobb. The Pirates were just one win away from sending the Tigers to another World Series defeat. But the Tigers were game, and in the next contest back at home they battered Willis again, scoring in the first, fourth, fifth, and sixth innings. Of the ten hits the Tigers collected in their 5–4 Game 6 win, Cobb had one, a run-scoring double. The victory set up a decisive seventh game in Detroit, the first time the modern World Series had advanced to a winner-take-all contest. But the game proved to be anticlimactic, as the Pirates pounded Bill Donovan and George Mullin, to win easily 8–0. Adams was brilliant in winning his third game over the Tigers, allowing just six hits while shackling Cobb 0 for 4. The Pittsburgh Pirates were world champions, and the Tigers were left to contemplate their fate as three-time losers of the World Series.

The battle between Cobb and Wagner had proved to be a mismatch. Wagner hit .333 with 3 extra-base hits, 6 RBIs, 4 runs scored, and 6 steals. Cobb had belted 3 doubles but hit just .231 (6 for 26) with a pair of steals and 5 RBIs. His career record in World Series play showed a .262 average on 17 hits in 65 at-bats, with 4 doubles, 1 triple, 0 homers, 9 RBIs, 7 runs scored, and 6 stolen bases. The Tigers failure in this Series had come down to two factors: the pitching of Babe Adams, and the failure of Detroit catchers to halt Pittsburgh's running game. The Pirates had swiped 14 bases on catchers Boss Schmidt and Oscar Stanage.

The Series had been a huge success at the gate, drawing a record number of fans. Each Tiger earned $1,273.50 in World Series shares, a handsome sum to supplement their regular season salary. Cobb's salary was about to take a sharp upswing, as he and Navin had already come to agreement for the 1910 campaign. Cobb signed a three-year deal paying him $9,000 per season plus a bonus if he won the batting title. It was more money than any other player in the American League would earn for the 1910 season, and only Honus Wagner was making more in all of professional baseball.

Despite the loss in the World Series, Cobb's daring style of baseball excited fans all over the league. Though he had few friends on his own team, he had earned their respect. Never again would he be tormented by taunts or insults from inside his own clubhouse. With three straight American League flags to their credit, the Tigers had assembled a group of talented players around their young batting champion. But although the years ahead would provide phenomenal personal success for Ty, his team would never advance to the World Series again during Cobb's career.

NOTES

1. Sam Crawford file, National Baseball Hall of Fame Library.

2. Lawrence S. Ritter, oral history interview with Sam Crawford (March 27, 1964), National Baseball Hall of Fame Library.

3. Schoor, *The Story of Ty Cobb*, 59.

4. Alexander, *Ty Cobb*, 112.

5. Cobb, with Stump, *My Life in Baseball, the True Record*, 65.

6. Ibid.

7. *Washington Star*, July 14, 1907, 20.

8. Dave Anderson, *Pennant Races: Baseball At Its Best* (New York: Galahad Books, 1997), 26.

9. Nap Rucker file, National Baseball Hall of Fame Library.

10. *Detroit Free Press*, June 22, 1908.

11. Cobb, with Stump, *My Life in Baseball*, 76.

12. The loss proved so shocking to the Naps that their former owner, Frank DeHaas Robison, listening to the game via telephone in suburban Cleveland, suffered a heart attack and died hours later.

13. Anderson, *Pennant Races*, 34.

14. McCallum, *The Tiger Wore Spikes*, 49.

15. *Detroit Free Press*, August 8, 1908, 1–2.

16. Alexander, *Ty Cobb*, 73.

17. Frederick G. Lieb, *Connie Mack: Grand Old Man of Baseball* (New York: G. P. Putnam's Sons, 1945), 37.

18. Ty Cobb file, National Baseball Hall of Fame Library.

19. Alexander, *Ty Cobb*, 91.

20. *Philadelphia Inquirer*, September 17, 1909, 5.

21. *Detroit Free Press*, unknown date, clipping from Ty Cobb player file, National Baseball Hall of Fame Library.

22. Ibid.

"BRAINS IN HIS FEET"

Just four days after the conclusion of the 1909 World Series, Ty Cobb voluntarily surrendered himself to police in Cleveland, under the charges stemming from the incident with the security guard at the Hotel Euclid in September. Accompanied by Frank Navin and his lawyers, Cobb pleaded not guilty to the charge of felonious assault and paid his release on bond. The trial was set for November, with Navin and Cobb anxious to clear the matter up before the 1910 season. On November 22, Cobb returned to Cleveland for the trial to find that Navin had successfully plea-bargained the charges down to simple assault and battery. Ty appeared in front of the judge, pled guilty and accepted a $100 fine. With the ugly incident behind him, Cobb returned to Augusta, where he and his wife spent the winter at the Oaks, the Lombard's sprawling estate south of the city. In December, a reception at the Oaks in honor of Ty's third consecutive batting championship attracted more than 200 family members, friends, and local officials. While in Augusta, Cobb enjoyed playing golf at the Augusta Country Club. For a short time he also lent his name to the Ty Cobb Tire Company.

During the winter of 1909–1910, Ty and Charlotte Cobb were expecting their first child. At the Oaks, on January 30, a boy—Tyrus Raymond Cobb Jr.— was born. Cobb was delighted with the arrival of a son, who was surrounded by the Roswell clan as well as Ty's mother and sister, who spent much of the winter in Augusta visiting the newborn. Ty and Charlotte later welcomed a daughter, Shirley, in 1911, and another son, Roswell Herschel, in 1916.

In March, with the Tigers once again in San Antonio, Cobb delayed his arrival until the last week of spring training. On April 7, Charlotte and their new son joined Ty en route to Detroit, where three days later the 1910 season began against Cleveland. The Tigers were the favorites to win their fourth straight American League pennant, and after two losses to the Naps to begin the season, they rallied for eight victories in nine games to take their customary spot at the top of the standings on April 29. The Tigers, as was their custom, had kept their team intact. Although Jennings had decided that Davy Jones was his everyday left fielder in place of Matty McIntyre and a few of the bench players were new, the remainder of the squad filled out as it had at the end of 1909. Cobb, at 23 years old, was the second youngest regular on the team, just one year older than shortstop Donie Bush, who was fast becoming his closest friend in the big leagues. In spite of his youth, Cobb demanded and received respect from most of his teammates, some of whom grudgingly ignored their contempt for the southerner and acknowledged his greatness on the diamond.

Having won three consecutive batting titles while leading his team to three consecutive pennants, Cobb seemed more confident early in 1910 than in any previous season. In April, he hit .396 in 12 games with 7 stolen bases; in May he batted .379; and in June he collected 40 hits in 26 games to lift his average to .395. But even though he swiped an amazing 18 bases and hit .390 in July, the Tigers 14–14 mark that month left them far behind the red-hot Athletics. Less important, but still of concern to Cobb, was the fact that he was more than twenty points behind Cleveland's Nap Lajoie in the batting race. Lajoie, a solid right-handed hitter with quick wrists, was enjoying a remarkable season, with his average up near the .425 mark.

In August, with the Tigers out of the race, Cobb's unpredictable temper flared once again. After he and Jones argued over a missed hit-and-run sign, Cobb responded by sulking for two days, refusing to report to the clubhouse. He watched the Tigers from the Bennett Park grandstands, until on August 6, he returned after apologizing to Jennings. That same day, which was Cobb's first wedding anniversary, Ty was involved in an incident with some rowdy fans in the outfield. Playing center field, Cobb withstood several innings of abuse from Detroit fans who were giving him a hard time for missing a few games. Finally, in the seventh inning, Cobb had heard enough and climbed into the outfield bleachers to confront the fans, who had been hurling obscenities at him. As he waded into the crowd he became embroiled in a shouting match with a black man and had to be restrained from attacking the spectator.

Gradually, as the season wore on and it became apparent that Detroit would not repeat as league champions, Cobb and his teammates began to butt heads. Crawford and Jones, his outfield partners, complained that Ty was more interested in winning the batting title than helping the team win. With the Chalmers

Automobile Company having promised a new roadster to whomever won the batting title, there was more on the line than bragging rights. The controversy shook Cobb enough that he hit just .290 in August, still trailing Lajoie in the batting race. On the first of September, Lajoie had dropped to .377, with Ty's mark resting well within striking distance at .372. Later in the month, after a 5-for-6 performance against the Highlanders, Cobb surpassed Lajoie, but the drama was far from over.

On October 1, Cobb went 1 for 3, and the next afternoon he collected four hits in a 12–7 win over the Browns. When he rapped out seven hits in his next four games, Cobb held a comfortable eight-point lead over Lajoie in the batting race. With two games left against the White Sox, and confident that he would once again cop the title, Cobb left the team in Chicago, met his wife and son in Detroit, and departed for Philadelphia, where he would play in a series of exhibition games. On the final day of the season, Lajoie and his team played a double-header against the Browns, who were managed by Jack O'Connor. Prior to the game, O'Connor let his team know how much he'd like to see Lajoie beat out Cobb for the batting title and the free automobile.

In Lajoie's first at-bat, he lined a fly ball to center field over the head of rookie Hub Northen, who was playing so shallow he could practically shake hands with the infield. Lajoie had a triple. The next time up, Lajoie bunted to the left of the pitching mound, where Browns shortstop Bobby Wallace casually retrieved the ball and threw late to first base. The official scored called it a hit. His next time to the plate, Lajoie bunted toward third, where John "Red" Corriden was stationed so far back he was practically in short left field. Corriden, no fan of Cobb's and a good friend of O'Connor's, was in on the shenanigans. Lajoie bunted to third six more times in the double-header, collecting a total of eight hits in nine at-bats. Harry Howell, a former pitcher serving as a coach under O'Connor, wasn't satisfied with Lajoie's near perfect day. Howell attempted to bribe the official scorer with the promise of a new suit of clothes if he would give Lajoie a ninth hit in Game Two, but was unsuccessful. The St. Louis fans were so pleased with Lajoie's performance that they surrounded the popular player after the game and offered their congratulations. Back in Chicago, hearing the news of Lajoie's eight-hit game, several of Cobb's teammates, who were bristling at Ty's early departure, sent a telegram of congratulations to Lajoie. Everyone thought that Lajoie had won the batting title.

It didn't take long for the dubious details of the game to reach the ears of American League president Ban Johnson. Several sportswriters covering the game had sent their eyewitness accounts to the league office. Meanwhile, O'Connor, Howell, Corriden, and even Lajoie, maintained an air of innocence. Citing his several bunt hits, Lajoie said, "I fooled them right along." But Johnson was not fooled. He ordered the league statisticians to give Cobb credit for a suspended game earlier in the season, in which Ty had went 1 for 2. When the final averages were released, Lajoie's 8-for-9 performance was counted, but Cobb's batting average was still slightly higher: .384944 to .384084.[1]

Johnson ordered the Browns to fire both O'Connor and Howell, which they did within a few days. Oddly, Corriden—the third baseman who had followed O'Connor's orders and let Lajoie bunt away—was not disciplined. Two years later he would be Cobb's teammate on the Tigers.

With a brand new Chalmers automobile and a fourth straight batting title, Cobb was personally satisfied with his 1910 season. He had led the league in slugging and runs scored, and owned a dazzling .347 career batting average. But it had been a disappointing season for the Detroit Tigers, who finished a distant third to Connie Mack's Athletics. The A's would play the National League champion Chicago Cubs in the World Series, but because it wouldn't start for another week, Cobb and several other American League stars played in a series of exhibition games in Philadelphia. Cobb's teammates included Walter Johnson, Addie Joss, Tris Speaker, Clyde Milan, and other AL notables.

After the exhibition series concluded, Cobb covered the World Series for the *Detroit Free Press*, and then left for Augusta with his wife and son. He was looking forward to a rest in Georgia after a trying season that saw him battle his teammates as well as spectators and opposing teams. That off-season Cobb took time from his relaxation to embark on a new hobby: auto racing. The thrill of speed that racing provided enticed Cobb, but after thinking over the possible damage he could inflict to his valuable baseball-playing body, he gave it up.

In November, Cobb and several other Tiger players took part in a series of exhibition games in Cuba against a group of professional Latin and African American players. For the first time in his life, Cobb played on a field against players of color. Many of the players he faced were Latin-born, but some were African Americans who had come south after the Negro leagues' season had ended in the United States. Major league baseball in 1910 was segregated, and had been for more than fifteen years. Black ballplayers had their own leagues, though they were more apt to splinter and disintegrate, due to lack of money. Many of the ballplayers in those leagues were very talented, however. In Cuba, Ty played against legendary black stars such as shortstop John Henry "Pop" Lloyd (who was known as the "Black Honus Wagner"), and Bruce Petway, a fine catcher with an excellent arm. In one game, Cobb was thrown out by Petway trying to steal second base by several feet. In another contest, Cobb was caught in a run-down between home and third before Petway applied a tag. Sufficiently motivated to showcase his skills to Petway and the others, Cobb hit 3 triples in the final two games of the series. Regardless, Lloyd and Petway, as well as Grant

Johnson, an African American infielder, out-hit Cobb during the exhibition. It was the last time Cobb ever competed with players of color.

During the off-season, Cobb continued his regiment to strengthen his legs, wearing weights in his boots as he traipsed through the woods. In 1911 the Tigers trained in Monroe, Louisiana. Cobb reported late and then departed on his own for Detroit in early April, wishing to forego the customary exhibition tour.

The season opened on April 13, against the White Sox at Bennett Park, which had been enlarged to hold more than 13,000 fans. The Tigers were once again built around the same key figures: Cobb, Crawford, and Jones in the outfield, Bush and George Moriarty on the left side of the infield, and Mullin, Ed Willett, Ed Summers, and Bill Donovan on the mound. Absent was Boss Schmidt, Cobb's old fighting buddy, who had been given his release.

Detroit won their fist six games of the season, as Cobb and Crawford both flexed their batting muscle early. By May 19, the "Bengals," as scribes were calling them, sported an impressive 27–5 record, and were 9½ games ahead of their closest competitors. Cobb was hitting .420 at that juncture, with 21 stolen bases and 47 runs scored. "The Georgia Peach," just 24 years old, was on the way to his greatest season.

The American League had introduced a new, cork-centered baseball for the 1911 season, and a few weeks into the schedule, fans, writers, and players realized it was a revolutionary decision. In 1910, the league batting average had been .243. In 1911, it would jump thirty points to .273. The impact was immediate. Where once the pitchers had dominated and 1–0 and 2–1 games were commonplace, now teams were piling up runs. No team took advantage of the new baseball more than the Detroit Tigers, who fielded several of the best hitters in the league.

But Cobb's skills went far beyond hitting the baseball. On the basepaths he was nearly impossible to contain. In one game he stole second, third, and home on successive pitches, announcing his intentions prior to each play. On another occasion, Cobb scored from second base on a sacrifice bunt, stunning the opposing catcher. Another time, Cobb scored from second base on a fly ball, prompting a New York scribe to write: "In base running Cobb slides at every opportunity, with a wiggly, fade-away twist that makes him as elusive as an eel."[2] He swiped third base as easily as other players took second base, beating opposing catcher's throws with a cloud of dust and a flash of his spikes. Umpire Bill McGowan said of him: "He could win a game without swinging a bat. He'd come up swinging five bats, smacking his lips like a tiger, and scaring the life out of a pitcher. He'd coax a pass, steal second, third, and home, and beat you, 1–0."[3]

In 1911, Cobb's daring as a base runner came into synch with his phenomenal batting ability, and what transpired was one of the greatest seasons in baseball history. On May 15, Cobb went 2 for 4 against "Smokey" Joe Wood of the Red Sox. The next day he went 3 for 5, and after that he proceeded to get a hit in every game for seven weeks. His hitting streak of forty games was a new American League record. During the streak he hit a blistering .476 (80 for 168) with 40 runs scored. He recorded 26 multiple-hit games during the streak, and never went more than two at-bats without reaching base via a hit or a walk. Finally, on July 4th, in the first game of a double-header against the White Sox in Detroit, Ed Walsh halted Ty's streak. In the second game, Ty lined collected two singles and proceeded to hit safely in fourteen of his next sixteen games.

By the middle of the season, Cobb was on a pace to break the all-time record for runs scored, hits, and batting average. Sportswriter E. A. Batchelor placed Ty on a lofty perch: "In my considered opinion, he was, all things considered, the greatest ball player that ever lived and the most valuable piece of property ever owned by any ball club."[4]

Cobb's base running techniques were revolutionary. Noticing that he lost precious strides when he rounded the bases widely, Cobb set out to shorten his path to home plate. When he would round third he would plant his left foot on the inside corner of the base and catapult himself toward home in a virtual straight line. This method served another important strategic purpose: by running as squarely as he could down the baseline, he presented an obstacle to third basemen trying to throw to the plate. Many times a ball would ricochet harmlessly off Cobb, allowing him to glide in with the run. One opposing AL manager said of Cobb, "I believe he carries brains in his feet. At least he plays that way."[5]

As he terrorized the league with his bat and his legs, rumors began to circulate that Cobb had a secret weapon in store for enemy infielders. "I didn't walk any closer than 50–60 yards from him," infielder Frank Ellerbe said, "but I went out to the ball park there in Detroit one day and I saw him sitting over there—and it looked to me certainly that he had a file filing his spikes."[6] Throughout his career, Cobb did little to dispel the rumors, and he stubbornly maintained that the basepaths belonged to the runner.

With his batting average in the rarified air of the .440 mark, Cobb became ill in August—most likely from exhaustion—and missed four games against Chicago. When he returned he was refreshed, piling up four consecutive multiple-hit games. On August 22, at home against the Highlanders, Cobb was ejected for arguing balls and strikes. Detroit lost the game—their fourteenth defeat in twenty-one games. Their once large lead was now a deficit, as they trailed the Athletics by four and one-half games at the conclusion of August. Cobb did his best to rally the team in September, stringing together a sixteen-game hitting streak that kept his average near the .420 mark. But Philadelphia continued to win, going 21–6 in September to wrap up the pennant. The Tigers limped to a second place finish, thirteen and one-half games back of the "Mackmen."

Unlike the previous season, when Cobb had earned the wrath of his teammates for what they deemed his "selfish pursuit of the batting title," Ty was a more mature ballplayer in 1911:

> Ty Cobb is a pretty good fellow. . . . Talk to a lot of people and they will tell you that this great speeder thinks of nothing else outside of his own fine average, his daily egregious stunts and such. . . . Cobb is nothing of an egotist, as a lot of fans like to make him out. The best thing a ball player can do is to recognize his constituents and at all times make friendly with them. Well, one Tyrus has gone a little bit further than that. He has gone so far as to show magnanimity by explaining to several of the other players how to play the game like he does. Joe Jackson, the Cleveland player, is second to Cobb in base stealing, and many think that the lessons taught to the Nap by Ty are responsible for this. If reports are correct, Ty showed Joe how to use the fade away slide and also pointed out the other fine points of base running.[7]

Amazingly, Cobb declined to play the last four games of the schedule, preferring to get an early start on his off-season. Had he played he likely would have added to his staggering 1911 numbers: 248 hits (a new major league record), 147 runs scored, 47 doubles, 24 triples, 8 homers, 127 RBIs, and 83 stolen bases. The latter figure was a new league record. Cobb's .420 batting average secured his fifth straight batting title, and it placed him in the exclusive circle of .400 hitters.

In November, Cobb joined the list of ballplayers turned actor. At that time, several baseball stars earned extra money in the off-season as actors in vaudeville plays and silent film. "Turkey Mike" Donlin was the most famous baseball player to try a career on the stage, having abandoned his playing career in 1908. Though he had no previous acting experience, Cobb accepted the lead role in George Ade's play *The College Widow*, a popular comedy of that era, which was later the inspiration for the Marx Brothers' screen hit *Horse Feathers*. Cobb played "Billy Bolton," a football-playing collegian in his fourth year as a freshman at college. For his role in the play, which toured the country, Cobb earned a reported $8,400—nearly as much as his baseball contract netted him in one season. His reviews were mostly favorable, but when a theater critic in Georgia gave him a bad review, Cobb responded with venom. "I am a better actor than you are, a better sports editor than you are, a better dramatic critic than you are. I make more money than you do, and I know I am a better ball player—so why should inferiors criticize superiors?"[8]

In the second week of January 1912, Cobb quit the play and returned to Detroit to join his family. A report from New York stated: "Today will mark the retirement of Ty Cobb from the stage for all time. The Georgia phenomenon was booked up to the time the Tigers start for their Dixie training camp, but he says he has had enough now."[9]

In Detroit, Cobb checked on the construction of the Tigers new ballpark, to be named Navin Field. The park was a steel-and-concrete structure with all the modern amenities of the era. Built on the same site as Bennett Park, at the intersection of Michigan and Trumbull Avenues in downtown Detroit, Navin Field could hold 23,000 spectators and had the finest playing surface in the big leagues. Also, for the first time, the Tigers would have dugouts and clubhouses for both the home and visiting teams.

But outside of the debut of their new ballpark, 1912 was a dismal season for the Detroit Tigers. Hampered by injuries and inconsistent pitching, the team dropped to sixth place with a dreadful 69–84 record. Their years of standing pat with the same players had caught up with them.

On April 20, 1912, as the country was reeling from the sinking of the H.M.S. *Titanic*, Navin Field was opened to a standing-room crowd of 24,389. Cobb was brilliant in the new park, lining two singles and making a spectacular catch in deep center field. Twice in the game, which Detroit won 6–5, Cobb was safe on the front end of a double steal. The second time he turned the trick, Cobb swiped home. Five days later, Cobb blasted the first home run in the new park, victimizing Earl Hamilton of the St. Louis Browns. On May 9, against Charley "Sea Lion" Hall, Cobb became the first player to homer in another brand-new venue—the Red Sox' Fenway Park. Opened on the same day as Navin Field, Fenway was nestled in the cozy neighborhoods of residential Boston.

On May 15, Cobb and the Tigers were in New York playing the third game of a four-game set with the Highlanders. During the game a rowdy fan named Claude Lueker, who had lost one hand and three fingers on the other hand in a printing press accident, heckled Cobb continuously. The heckling was so bad that at one point in the game Cobb decided to stand in a tunnel in deep center field rather than walk back to the Tiger bench to face more torment from Lueker. Later in the game, Cobb attempted to have Lueker thrown out of the park, but was unable to locate an official. Finally, Lueker increased his verbal attack, calling Cobb a "half-nigger." When teammates asked the increasingly agitated Cobb if he was going to stand for the abuse, Cobb leapt into the stands, charged at Lueker and began beating him with his fists. When Lueker fell on his back, Cobb began kicking him in the arms and head. When a nearby fan yelled that Lueker was handicapped, Cobb shouted, "I don't care if he has no feet." A report in the *Philadelphia Public Ledger* stated that Lueker's handicap left him "unable to defend himself properly against Cobb's swift blows."[10]

Umpire Frank "Silk" O'Loughlin and a policeman finally pulled Cobb off the battered Lueker. Ty was ejected from the game but remained on the Tiger bench until a few innings later when he walked across the field to get to the visitors' clubhouse. The New York crowd responded with an equal amount of cheering and booing.

Lueker later provided his version of the fracas. He claimed that he'd been one of many fans sitting in that section of the park who had hurled insults at Cobb, and that the Tiger star had unfairly targeted him as the culprit. "I did no more," Lueker pleaded later, "or said no more than a hundred or so persons who were seated about me."[11]

Cobb later recalled: "in New York I went into the grandstand after a fan who had called me every name that is unprintable. I hit him a couple of times and was again abused on all sides for being rowdy. Now no man could have stood the abuse heaped on me that day."[12]

His manager and teammates agreed, offering support when questioned about the incident after the game, which Detroit won 8–4. Unfortunately for Cobb, league president Ban Johnson had been in the stands and had witnessed the spectacle. That evening, Cobb met with Johnson and told his version of the story. The next day, Johnson suspended Cobb indefinitely. Newspaper coverage at the time overwhelmingly supported Cobb, citing the obscene heckling as ample cause for retaliation. Though few condoned Cobb's vicious physical attack on Leuker, they understood his motivation.

On May 17 in Philadelphia, Detroit defeated the A's by the score of 6–3, with Cobb watching from the stands. That evening every member of the team signed a telegram that was sent to Johnson demanding Cobb's reinstatement. The message, drafted by Davy Jones, threatened a player strike if their center fielder was not allowed to play immediately: "Feeling Mr. Cobb is being done an injustice by your action in suspending him, we, the undersigned, refuse to play in another game after today until such action is adjusted to our satisfaction. He was fully justified in his action as no one could stand such personal abuse from any one. We want him reinstated for tomorrow's game or there will be no game. If players' cannot have protection, we must protect ourselves."[13]

It was a rare case of Cobb's teammates rallying to his defense, and it proved historic. The next day the team showed up at Shibe Park expecting to play the Athletics with Cobb in the line-up. When the umpires followed the league mandate and ordered Cobb from the field, the entire Tigers team marched away with him. For the first time in baseball history, a team was on strike. Tigers infielder Jim Delahanty was dramatic in his support of Cobb: "A murderer is given a chance and a baseball player isn't. The assassin who shot President McKinley was given a trial. Cobb was suspended but he was afforded no opportunity for explaining. . . ."[14]

Hughie Jennings scrambled to avoid a forfeit. He and Navin had prepared for the possibility of a walkout and had secured a dozen Philadelphia sandlot players to take the field if necessary. For the chance to earn $10 a piece (to Navin, a small price to pay compared with a potential $1,000 fine from the league for not playing the game), the amateurs took the field against the A's.

Before a puzzled crowd of more than 14,000 fans, the A's bombarded their inexperienced and outmatched foes 24–2, with Eddie Collins collecting five hits and five stolen bases. The makeshift Tiger line-up included 20-year old pitcher Aloysius Travers, who went the distance, surrendering all 24 runs, only 14 of which were earned. The right-hander walked seven batters and somehow managed to strike out one. Forty-eight-year-old coach Deacon McGuire caught and collected a single in the farce, and Jennings inserted himself as a pinch-hitter late in the blowout.

The stubborn Tigers regulars had exhibited solidarity while at the same time aggravating president Johnson. The *Philadelphia Public Ledger* claimed that "the mutiny against the authority of Johnson is one of the biggest sensations in baseball in recent years. Never before has a team of ball players dared to question the authority or judgment of President Johnson."[15]

Two days later, after canceling the final game of the series, Johnson met with the striking players and demanded their return. He threatened to throw them out of Organized Baseball if they failed to capitulate. Urged by Cobb, the players backed down. Johnson slapped each of them with a fine and suspended Cobb for ten days, retroactive to the day of his ejection in New York. He also fined Cobb fifty dollars half the amount he penalized the striking players.

On May 26, Cobb was back in the line-up with his .360 batting average. Before long, the Leuker incident was behind him and Cobb was back in the groove. On June 7, against Boston he stole three bases in a 4–3 victory. On June 14 at home against the A's, Cobb banged out three hits and drove in every run in a 4–3 Detroit victory. In July, as the weather heated up, so did the Georgia Peach. In that month he was held hitless in just one game, and on the nineteenth against the Athletics in Philadelphia, he went 5 for 5 with two homers off Carroll "Boardwalk" Brown. During that six-game series with Connie Mack's squad, which consisted of three consecutive double-headers, Cobb went 18 for 27, with 3 doubles, 3 triples, and 2 home runs. It was one of the greatest stretches of hitting anyone had ever seen, and it was prompted in part by Cobb's rage over the poor treatment that Philadelphia fans had given him over the years. Speaking to George "Stoney" McLinn, sports editor of the *Philadelphia Press* and a founder of the Baseball Writers' Association of America, Cobb boasted: "I am going to get more hits than anybody ever got before in six straight games. Be sure and come out and see me show your Quaker fans what I can do when they get me mad."[16] Later in the month, Cobb strung together seven straight multiple-hit games, raising his average to .426 on the season. He was on the way to his sixth consecutive batting title.

Then in August Cobb was involved in yet another violent encounter. On the evening of August 11, while driving with his wife to the train station to meet his teammates, Cobb was assaulted by three men. When Cobb halted his Chalmers to help the men, who were pretending to be in distress, they attacked him and dragged him from the car. While his wife watched in horror, Cobb battled the trio, one of whom pulled a knife. During the melee, Cobb was slashed across his back with the knife. Despite the wound, he chased two of the men to a nearby alley and beat them with the revolver he carried in his suit pocket. One of the men lay in a pool of blood at the dark end of the alley after suffering several blows to the head.

When Cobb met his team at the train station he was patched up by the team trainer and was in the line-up for an exhibition game against Syracuse of the New York State League the next day. He collected three hits to delight a crowd of fans in Syracuse. Years later, Cobb recalled: "while driving my auto to the train in Detroit, I was set on by three men and stabbed in the back. I never have been able to solve this mystery. Why they did this no one knows."[17] At the time of the attack, a few newspapers speculated that the incident was payback for Cobb's beating of Lueker. Whatever the motive, Cobb had survived yet another brutal struggle.

Cobb continued to hit well as the 1912 season closed, buoyed by a fourteen-game hitting streak in September. His final numbers for 1912 were once again spectacular: a .410 batting average, 227 hits, 119 runs scored, 23 triples, and 61 stolen bases. He had been a daredevil on the bases, having stole home eight times, including three times against Cleveland.

When the season closed on October 6, Cobb was already on his way to New York to cover the upcoming World Series for a newspaper syndicate. It was another way for Cobb to garner some extra cash. Like baseball, earning money was something that Cobb excelled at. A shrewd businessman, in 1918 Cobb bought his first stock in Coca-Cola, an Atlanta-based soft drink company, and continued to invest in Coca-Cola throughout his lifetime. Cobb also invested wisely in General Motors, beginning in 1913. Cobb's investments paid off handsomely, helping to make him one of the first athletes to become independently wealthy.

In sharp contrast to other athletes who squandered their money and retired broke, Cobb built an enormous fortune over the course of his playing career and beyond. Later in his career, Cobb gave his teammates stock tips. Hall of Fame second baseman Charlie Gehringer recalled that Cobb would give the younger players financial advice. "He told us about Coca-Cola and egged us on to buy the stock, but we weren't making enough money to buy shares."[18]

Following the 1912 season, Cobb's three-year, $9,000-per-year contract had elapsed. Navin was anxious to secure Cobb's signature on a Detroit contract, but as in 1909, Cobb held out for more money. A six-time batting champion, Cobb wanted $15,000 per year for three years. He wanted security for himself and his family.

In March, while the rest of the Tigers reported to spring training in Gulfport, Mississippi, Cobb held out, staying back in Augusta. For the next month, Cobb and Navin slung insults at each other. On April 10, without Cobb in the line-up, the Tigers opened the 1913 season at St. Louis, losing 3–1. In typical fashion, most newspapers were anti-Cobb in the standoff. The *Sporting News* wrote that Cobb "has done more than any other individual to give enemies a chance to make attacks [against baseball]. But what does Cobb care? He is for Cobb. That is the way he plays the game whether it be on the field or in negotiating a contract."[19]

Finally, on April 24, Navin blinked. He begged Cobb to come to Detroit for salary negotiations, and within a few hours of face-to-face haggling, the two adversaries came to terms. Cobb would receive $12,000 for the 1913 season. He responded by telling reporters, "This is my last holdout."[20]

On April 29, when Cobb made his first appearance in a Detroit uniform in 1913, the Tigers had already played fourteen games. He went 1 for 4 with an RBI against the White Sox as the Tigers lost in extra innings. After coming down with the flu, Cobb was out of the line-up again. When he returned, he went hitless in his three straight games, the first time that had occurred since August of 1910. But then, as if challenged by some demon inside him, Cobb responded with 23 hits and a .622 average in his next 11 games. Over a three-game stretch against the Athletics, Cobb collected hits in seven straight at-bats.

But the Tigers were not faring as well. After losing to Doc White 3–2 on May 31, Detroit was in seventh place, fourteen games behind Philadelphia. The team was in a transitional phase, still clinging to a few players who were past their prime while also breaking in younger prospects. One of those promising young players was 25-year-old right fielder Bobby Veach, who was in his first full big-league season. Veach would play alongside Cobb in the Detroit outfield for eleven years, swinging a powerful bat and flashing a strong arm. Middle infielder Ossie Vitt was also breaking in on the team, while several veterans were on their last legs. George Mullin, a dependable member of Detroit's rotation since 1902, would start seven games for Jennings in 1913 before being waived. His place was taken by George "Hooks" Dauss, a rookie curveball specialist.

In both June and July, Cobb suffered minor injuries which kept him out of the line-up for brief stretches. In August, he hit .466 over an eight-game stretch and drew nearer to batting leader Joe Jackson of Cleveland. When September began, Jackson was still eight points ahead of Cobb, but the Georgia Peach made his usual run at the crown, eventually overtaking Jackson when he batted .462 during a ten-game hitting streak that ended on September 17.

Cobb wrapped up his season by hitting safely in his final eleven games, which gave him an average of .390. He had garnered his seventh straight batting title, a major league record. His holdout and the injuries had kept him to just 122 games, and despite his lofty average, it had been his worst season since 1906. The Tigers finished in sixth place once again, several laps back of Connie Mack's Athletics.

In November, Ty and Charlotte, with their two young children, Tyrus Jr. and Shirley, moved into a home located in Augusta on Williams Street in the up-scale section of Augusta. Over the years Ty's spacious home in Augusta would be the scene of social gatherings that welcomed such notable visitors as Georgia Governor Joseph Mackey Brown, U.S. Congressman Carl Vinson, golfing legend Bobby Jones, college football coach Knute Rockne, composer John Philip Sousa, millionaire and Coca-Cola president Robert Woodruff, and sportswriter Grantland Rice. Throughout Cobb's life, as his stature and wealth rose with his batting average, he spent time in the company of many famous people. During the 1910s, he met Presidents Taft and Wilson, and in the 1920s he played cards with President Warren Harding, for whom he campaigned.

Not wanting to repeat the hostile holdout of the previous off-season, Cobb quickly agreed to contract terms with Detroit for 1914. He signed for $15,000, the figure he had asked of Navin the previous winter. Cobb wasn't aware of it at the time, but the salary was just the second-highest in baseball; Boston's Tris Speaker was earning $16,500.

Cobb's motivation for agreeing to a contract so quickly without a hassle was to avoid the negative reaction he'd received from his previous holdouts, but Navin's reason was more complicated. In 1914, the upstart Federal League would seriously threaten the American and National League markets. The Federal League was backed by wealthy owners who would sign several major league stars over the next two seasons, including Three Finger Brown, Hal Chase, Eddie Plank, and Joe Tinker. Even Walter Johnson, the best pitcher in baseball, was briefly seduced by the Federal League, signing a contract for the 1915 season before having a change of heart. In 1914, the Federal League cut into Major

League Baseball's business, as attendance dropped nearly 25 percent in the AL and NL.

When the Tigers broke spring training and headed north to start the 1914 campaign, they had several new faces on the team. There was a new right side of the infield: first baseman George Burns and second baseman Marty Kavanagh. New to the pitching staff was Harry Coveleski, a veteran left-hander in his second stint in the big leagues after a three-year hiatus in the minors. The only player who remained on the Tigers from Cobb's rookie season was Sam Crawford, who was still going strong, having hit .317 the previous year.

At Navin Field on April 14, in front of more than 21,000 fans, the Tigers opened the season with a 3–2 victory over the Browns, managed by Branch Rickey. Cobb went 1 for 5 with a triple in the opener. In 1914, Detroit had their best start in several seasons, winning ten of their first fourteen games. Despite mediocre success in the month of May, the Tigers were just one game back of Philadelphia and Washington, who were tied for first place. But Cobb was not with the team at that time. On May 19 in Boston, Cobb was struck by a pitch that cracked a rib in his right side. He missed more than two weeks of action, during which time the Tigers struggled to a 6–10 record. On June 6, Cobb returned with a vengeance: in his first twelve games back he hit .422 with 4 doubles. On June 20, the Tigers were one-half game behind the A's. Then Cobb became embroiled in another altercation that left his reputation and himself bloodied.

On the evening of June 20, Cobb and his dinner guest, Washington manager Clark Griffith, arrived at Ty's Detroit home to find Charlotte upset over an argument she'd had with their butcher earlier that day. Cobb quickly phoned the butcher, William Carpenter, and arranged to meet him at his shop. Cobb marched out of the house carrying his revolver, leaving the stunned Griffith and his wife behind. When Carpenter saw the pistol-carrying Cobb walk in, he quickly apologized and offered to apologize to Mrs. Cobb. But then, with the issue seemingly resolved, Carpenter's assistant, a black man named Harold Harding, appeared from the back of the store waving a butcher knife. Harding threatened Cobb and advanced toward him. Cobb slugged Harding and beat him over the head with his pistol while a rattled Carpenter phoned the police. When authorities arrived they arrested Cobb, and the ballplayer spent the evening in jail, nursing the broken thumb he'd suffered in the altercation. In the morning he was released when Harding decided not to file charges, but with the publicity over the fight and his broken thumb to contend with, Cobb's troubles were far from resolved. A few days later, Carpenter decided to press charges against Cobb, citing disturbance of the peace. After being arrested and posting bail, Cobb pleaded guilty and paid a fifty-dollar fine. Meanwhile the broken thumb kept him out of the line-up.

Following nearly six weeks on the sidelines, Cobb returned on August 7, hitting a pinch-hit triple off Boston's Vean Gregg in a 3–1 triumph at Navin Field. But Detroit had suffered greatly from his absence and was hopelessly out of the pennant race, thirteen games behind the A's.

With his season average at .340, Cobb was more than thirty points behind Joe Jackson for the batting title. But from that point on, Cobb hit .392 and once again eclipsed "Shoeless Joe" on his way to the crown. From August 27 to the first game of September 22, Cobb hit safely in twenty-three of twenty-five games, batting at a feverish .479 clip. But even though Cobb had won the batting title with a .368 average, for the second straight season he had failed to play enough games to lead the league in any cumulative category. He came to bat just 345 times, and stole just 35 bases in 97 games, his lowest output since 1906. Cobb had played ten seasons in the major leagues and won eight batting crowns. His career batting average was a stellar .369, the highest figure in the history of the game. He had helped the Tigers to three straight pennants from 1907 to 1909, but hadn't been able to help his team back to the World Series since.

During the winter of 1914–1915, Cobb contemplated his baseball future back in Augusta with his wife and their two children. When he wasn't hunting, Cobb worked on his legs, which he felt had started to betray him. The years of sliding and slashing his way around the bases had taken a toll. In December, Ty turned 28 years old, not old by any measure, but he'd been playing professional baseball longer than most players would their entire career. The average big leaguer spent three years at the top level and didn't arrive on the scene until he was 23 years old. Cobb had been with the Tigers since he was 18. His body, which he cared for meticulously, would need more attention in the coming years.

Indicating his determination to rebound from what he considered poor seasons in 1913 and 1914, Cobb reported on time to spring training in Gulfport, Mississippi, in March of 1915. For the first time in several years Cobb was in camp with the rest of his teammates for an entire spring training. Navin offered, and Cobb signed, a three-year deal worth $20,000 per year making him the highest paid player in the game. In camp that spring, Cobb got acquainted with Ralph "Pep" Young, the Tigers new second baseman, and William "Baby Doll" Jacobson, a rookie outfielder. Besides Young, Detroit's regulars for the 1915 campaign would be the same as the previous season: Oscar Stanage behind the plate, George "Tioga" Burns at first base, Ossie Vitt at third, Donie Bush at shortstop, Bobby Veach in left field, Cobb in center, and Crawford in right. Hooks Dauss,

Jean Dubuc, and Harry Covelski anchored the pitching staff, which also welcomed rookie Bernie Boland. After a fourth place finish in 1914, Jennings hoped to push his club back near the top of the American League standings. The Red Sox and A's figured to be the best teams in the loop.

As they had the previous season, the Tigers got off to a strong start in 1915. After losing to Cleveland on Opening Day in Detroit on April 14, they won nine of their next ten, including eight in a row. Helped by his aggressive off-season workouts, Cobb got out of the gate fast, hitting safely in the first ten games of the year while running with abandon on the basepaths. In two separate series against Cleveland (now known as the "Indians"), Cobb swiped seven bases off befuddled catcher Steve O'Neill. On May 11, the Tigers were in first place with an 18–7 record, three and one-half games in front of the surprising Yankees and White Sox. Cobb's batting average was well above the .400 mark, and his outfield mates, Crawford and Veach, were also hitting the ball well. With those three sluggers in the middle of their line-up, and with Cobb swiping bases and wreaking havoc on the diamond, the Tigers kept winning.

On May 11 in Detroit, Cobb faced a 20-year-old Boston pitcher named George Herman "Babe" Ruth for the first time. Cobb went 1 for 2 against the left-handed slants of Ruth, as the Tigers won 5–1. In early May, Cobb had another one of his hot streaks, batting .471 during an eight-game stretch, which also saw him pilfer 10 bases. On June 12 against Philadelphia, who had sunk to the bottom of the standings, Cobb stole four bases. It was the second time in the season that he had accomplished that feat against the A's. By the end of June it had become a three-team race, with the White Sox leading Detroit and Boston by five and one-half games.

Though Cobb was now coexisting peacefully with his teammates, he was still venomous to the opposition. On June 9 at Fenway Park, in a 15–0 rout of the Red Sox, Cobb slid hard into second base, spiking shortstop Everett "Deacon" Scott. Ignoring the angry reaction from the Boston fans, Cobb continued his harassment in a later game against the Red Sox, viciously spiking pitcher Hubert "Dutch" Leonard on a play at first base, after the hurler had brushed him back with a high fastball. On June 18, in Washington, Cobb, Veach, and Burns pulled a triple steal, with Ty sliding across home plate with a run; Senators catcher John "Bull" Henry was knocked unconscious on the play and had to leave the game. During the 1915 season, Cobb embodied his philosophy that "baseball is a red-blooded sport for red-blooded men. . . . a struggle for supremacy, survival of the fittest."[21]

Cobb displayed more daring base running during the 1915 season than in any other in his illustrious career. He stole home five times, including four times in June, when he swiped a total of 28 bases, a major league record for a single month. On June 23, against St. Louis, Cobb scored from second base on a ground ball hit to the pitcher by Crawford. While the opposing pitcher sat near the mound fumbling for the ball, Ty bolted around third and thundered down the baseline with the winning run. In July against the Athletics, Cobb doubled and stole third and then scored when he dashed for home on a pickoff attempt, sliding under the late relay throw from the third baseman.

In September against the Browns, Cobb's bold base running single-handedly defeated St. Louis, in a game that Browns manager Branch Rickey would never forget. In a tie game in the ninth inning, Cobb led off against southpaw Carl Weilman, who in eight years against Cobb held the batting champion to a modest .237 average. After heckling Weilman until he rattled the lefty, Cobb drew a base on balls. On first base, with the crowd yelling for him to steal, Cobb bounced off the bag, daring Weilman to throw over. The pitcher complied, firing several throws to first baseman John Leary, which chased Cobb back to the base. After one particular throw, Cobb taunted Weilman, daring him to throw it over one more time. Rickey stepped out of the visitor's dugout and ordered his pitcher to toss one more over to first. When he did, Cobb easily snapped back to the bag. But when Leary sloppily lopped the ball back to Weilman with a high arc, Cobb sped toward second base. Weilman hurried a throw to second base but the ball went into the dirt and bounced into center field. Cobb charged around second and headed toward third, where Jimmy Austin awaited the throw from the outfield. The throw arrived in plenty of time to nab Cobb, but Austin, fearing a jolting collision with Cobb, fumbled the ball. Then, as "Cobb did more thinking than the average player does in an entire season,"[22] Ty slid his right foot into the rolling baseball, kicking it into foul territory and toward the dugout. As Austin scrambled for the ball, Cobb glided home with the game-winning score. "That one play," Rickey said, "if nothing else, would convince me that Cobb was a super player."[23]

Cobb's antics on the base paths helped the Tigers stay in the pennant chase. In July the team went 19–9, and the next month they repeated that mark. Entering September, Detroit trailed the Red Sox by one and one-half games. Assessing the pennant race, Cobb said: "We have been playing the steadiest, the most consistent, ball of any club in the race since April. We haven't had any spurts nor any slumps. We have been merely moving along just a shade above .600. We are still due for a winning streak, and if a certain pair of pitchers [Bill James and Grover Lowdermilk] come to the help of Coveleski, Dauss and Dubuc, we'll get that streak and win. If they don't, Boston will win and we will finish second."[24] Despite a 10–5 mark in the first two weeks of September, the Tigers trailed Boston by two full games when the two teams met at Fenway Park for a crucial four-game series beginning on the sixteenth.

The bad blood between Cobb and the Boston pitching staff dated back several years, and had been heightened by Dutch Leonard's head-hunting earlier in the season. The animosity came to a head in the first game of the showdown. Throughout the contest Cobb was brushed back by tight pitches from Rube Foster and Carl Mays. Finally, Cobb was fed up, and in the eighth inning—after being knocked on the seat of his pants by a pitch aimed for his skull—Cobb hurled his bat toward Mays, who ducked for cover. On the very next pitch Mays hit Cobb in the wrist, prompting a near brawl, with Cobb hollering obscenities at Mays, the Boston bench, and the frenzied crowd. As he trotted to first base, Cobb was pelted with garbage thrown from the stands. Most appalling to the partisan Boston crowd was the fact that the Tigers built a 6–1 lead, which stood up as the final score.

When Cobb recorded the final put-out of the game, policemen were unable to keep the rowdy crowd from storming onto the field and surrounding Cobb in center. As most of his teammates retreated to safety, Cobb defiantly strolled through the sea of hateful fans, receiving their taunts and the barrage of garbage that was thrown at him. Sportswriter E. A. Batchelor, a witness to the incredible scene, wrote: "None of the mongrels in the crowd had the nerve to attack him—each waiting for somebody else to strike the first blow."[25]

After surviving the harrowing throngs of Boston fans in the opener, Cobb and the Tigers lost the last three games, placing them a distant four games behind the Red Sox. Though the Tigers would eventually end the season with a team-record 100 wins, they fell two and one-half games shy of first place. It was their best showing since their 1909 pennant-winning season.

Cobb had enjoyed one of his finest all-around seasons. The inconsistency of 1913–1914 had been erased by a season of daring and brilliance. Breaking a record he had shared with Honus Wagner, Cobb won his ninth consecutive batting title, hitting .369 with 208 hits. It was the fifth 200-hit season of his career. Cobb had stolen 96 bases, a major league record that would remain unchallenged for 47 years. His stolen base total was nearly twice that of the next highest figure in the American League (51 by Fritz Maisel). Cobb led the league in runs scored, having touched home plate 144 times. He also paced the league in total bases and ranked among the leaders in slugging, doubles, and RBIs. Also, for the first time in baseball history, three players from the same team had finished as the top three in the RBIs ranking, with Crawford (112), Veach (112) and Cobb (99) finishing in that order. Showing a willingness to be patient that helped him rack up his record stolen base total, Cobb walked 118 times, a figure nearly double his normal amount. Combining his walks, hits, and the ten times he was plunked by enemy pitchers, Cobb had reached base 336 times—an average of more than twice per game.

During the off-season, Cobb took time from his usual hunting excursions to visit the Hillerich and Bradbsy Bat Company in Louisville, Kentucky. Since 1884, when Pete Browning first used their product, Hillerich and Bradsby had supplied bats to major league players. Having won nine straight batting titles, Cobb was the company's most important client. Cobb toured the bat factory and hand-selected the lumber to be used for his bats. With a few dozen bats in tow, Cobb returned to Augusta, where he spent a peaceful winter with his family.

The most important baseball event that off-season was the collapse of the Federal League after two years of toe-to-toe competition with the American and National Leagues. In a last-ditch deal, Federal League club owners struck a deal which allowed a few of them to buy into the other two major leagues, and led to the signing of a handful of players who had gotten their start in the rebel circuit.

In late March of 1916, Cobb made his way to Waxahachie, a cotton-bearing Texas town located between Dallas and Waco, for spring training. The previous fall, the Tigers regular training site in Gulfport, Mississippi, had been damaged by a hurricane. The club looked much the same as it did the previous year, with Bill James, who had been acquired in the midst of the 1915 campaign, the one notable addition.

After a series of exhibition games as they traveled north, the Tigers opened the season at Chicago against the White Sox. Harry Coveleski, brother of future Hall of Fame hurler Stan, pitched a masterful 4–0 shutout for Detroit as Cobb delivered two hits. In the early going the team was streaky, losing four straight and then winning four in a row. Later in April, Cobb missed four games when he came down with a cold, but returned on the twenty-eighth with a 2 for 4 showing in a 6–5 win over the Browns. In early May, Jennings made an historic move when he shifted Crawford to a part-time role in favor of young Harry Heilmann. Heilmann had tasted a bit of big league action back in 1914, but after hitting .225, he spent the next season in the minor leagues. Given a chance by Jennings to play regularly in left field in 1916, Heilmann began an extremely successful 14-year stay in Detroit. With Bobby Veach still entrenched in right field, the Tigers had four talented outfielders, including Wahoo Sam in a part-time role.

Through the end of May, Ty was hitting a sluggish .327 with just 11 stolen bases. But the next month he caught fire, helping the team to get into the thick of the pennant race. For June he batted .384 and was back to his old methods on the bases. In six games in late June, he swiped 8 bases, including 3 in one contest against Cleveland. In a double-header on June 27 against St. Louis, Cobb stole 4 bases, including one steal of home. In total, the Georgia Peach recorded 18 steals in June of 1916, as the Tigers roared back into contention. The team was in sixth place, but they trailed the Yankees by just four and one-half games as several teams were bunched in the standings. Then in early July, Cobb was expelled from a game by home plate umpire Bill Nallin and subsequently suspended by Ban Johnson for three days. While the Tigers played a double-header against the Indians in Cleveland on July 4, Ty was at home in Augusta serving his suspension in the bosom of his family. Two days later, Cobb was back with the team in Philadelphia, where he pounded A's hurlers for 3 hits and 3 stolen bases. He added 5 more hits over the next two days, including a homer off Elmer Myers. Cobb seemed to have been rejuvenated by the three-day suspension, and hit .391 in his first 18 games back from the layoff, with 12 runs scored. After Detroit swept the A's, they took three of four from the Senators in Washington before splitting a six-game set with the Yankees at the Polo Grounds.

In August, the Tigers were helped by Cobb's four-hit game in a 9–0 win on August 8, and four straight multi-hit games by Ty a week later. The Tigers were slowly creeping up the standings. In late August, the Tigers won ten of eleven, including two over Boston at Fenway Park, where Cobb withstood a constant barrage of jeering from the Red Sox faithful. That surge left the Tigers a single game behind the Red Sox in the AL standings, with the White Sox not far behind. On September 3 at home against the Indians, Cobb helped the Tigers make ground in the pennant race. Ty went 4 for 4 with a double, a run scored, and a stolen base in a 5–3 win. After that performance, Tris Speaker, now playing for Cleveland, held a fourteen-point lead over Cobb in the batting race. A few weeks earlier, Cobb had trailed Speaker by close to thirty points.

On September 6, Cobb single-handedly defeated the Browns in extra innings at Navin Field. In the bottom of the tenth with one man out, Cobb beat out a slow roller for his third hit of the contest. On the first pitch to the next batter, Cobb took off for second base, sliding safely. When the throw from the Browns' catcher sailed into center field, Cobb popped up and strolled to third. Veach then lined a hard ground ball to first baseman George Sisler, who shot a glance at Cobb to force Ty to retreat to third base. But when Sisler put his head down and ran to first to retire Veach, Cobb streaked down the third baseline for home, sliding safely under Sisler's throw for the game-winning run.

A week later, at Cleveland, Cobb and Speaker met head-to-head. In that game, Ty cracked four hits, including two home runs, as Detroit romped to a 10–2 win. Showing his versatile talents, Cobb launched one homer deep over the right field fence, and hit another to left center for an inside-the-parker. After circling the bases with furious determination, Cobb slid into home with his famous fade-away technique, with only his left toe reaching back to touch home plate.

At the end of the second week of September, Detroit was one-half game behind the Red Sox, and Cobb was twelve points in back of Speaker. On September 13, a 4–1 gem by Coveleski vaulted the Tigers into a tie for first place, where they stayed for three days. When Howard Ehmke, a former Federal Leaguer, beat the A's on September 16, the Tigers were alone at the top of the standings. But the Red Sox and White Sox were both within a game of them. The next day, against Connie Mack's club, Cobb once again won a game in extra innings with his legs. With the score deadlocked 5–5 in the bottom of the tenth, Cobb coaxed a walked off "Bullet Joe" Bush. Dancing off first base, Cobb bolted to second when Veach dropped down a sacrifice bunt. When the throw to first to retire Veach was a little high, Cobb kept running and slid safely into third. When Heilmann hit a fly to left field, Cobb easily scored the game-winning run, keeping the Tigers a full game in front.

But within a few days the Tigers hopes for a fourth pennant in the Cobb era were destroyed. After losing the series finale to the A's on September 18, Detroit hosted the Red Sox for three weekday games at Navin Field. With close to 50,000 fans in attendance for the series, Detroit was swept by the Red Sox. Boston pitching, led by Carl Mays, Dutch Leonard, and finally Babe Ruth, held the potent Bengal offense in check, surrendering just six runs in the series. A few days later, Washington eliminated the Tigers from the race, pounding Hooks Dauss in an 8–5 slugfest.

All that was left for Cobb was his pursuit of Speaker and a tenth straight batting title, but that goal met a similar fate. On September 24, Cobb went 4 for 4 and gained eight points in the batting race, but even his frantic 17 for 27 stretch to end the season was too late to close the gap. Speaker had broken Cobb's iron-grip on the batting championship, winning with a .386 mark to Cobb's .371. Not since he was a teenager had Cobb played a season where he did not win a batting title.

Cobb's inconsistency early in the season had proved fatal, allowing Speaker to build an insurmountable lead. Cobb's final totals of 113 runs scored and 68 stolen bases paced the league, and once again he collected more than 200 hits, with a tally of 201. But most importantly to Ty, he had helped the Tigers stay in a pennant race most of the season. Though they had fallen short, Detroit was back in position to contend with Boston and Chicago for American League supremacy.

While Cobb and Detroit battled for the AL pennant at the end of the 1916 season, Charlotte Cobb had delivered Ty's third child, a son named Roswell Herschel. Cobb traveled home to Augusta to visit his wife and the new baby at the conclusion of the season. Later in October, Cobb participated in a series of exhibition games, playing with members of the world champion Boston Red Sox in New York, Connecticut, New Jersey, and other locations on the east coast.

The games were played against local semi-pro and minor league clubs, drawing good crowds in cities like Albany, Hartford, and Newark.

Following the exhibition schedule, which netted Cobb more than $800, Ty traveled to New York City, where he joined the Sunbeam Motion Picture Company to perform in a movie. Ty had been recruited by his friend Vaughn Glaser, a stage actor whom Cobb had met while performing in *The College Widow* in 1912. In *Somewhere in Georgia*, Cobb played a ballplayer who signs with the Detroit Tigers and later runs into trouble with a man who is courting the same woman he is. At the conclusion of the film, Cobb escapes from the bad guys and wins the girl. The film was not well received, nor was it particularly successful, but it was an historical piece of film history. It was the first motion picture featuring an actual athlete as the star, and it was the first widely distributed baseball movie.

That off-season the biggest story in America was the war in Europe, which was in its third year. President Woodrow Wilson was narrowly reelected in November behind the slogan "He Kept Us Out Of War!"—but the mood in the country was changing. Thousands of citizens who opposed Wilson's policies of isolationism had marched in cities across the nation in 1916. Meanwhile there was more unrest overseas. Early in 1917, a revolution in Russia led the ouster of Czar Nicholas II and eventually the rise of the communists. Shortly, the "Great War" would intrude on American life, including the game of baseball. The life of Ty Cobb, the national pastime's biggest star, would also be upturned.

NOTES

1. Based on statistics from Elias Stats, Inc., the official statistician of Major League Baseball.
2. "Naps Defeat the Tigers in Ninth," *New York Times*, May 30, 1911, 28.
3. *Sporting News*, July 5, 1950, 16.
4. Ty Cobb file, National Baseball Hall of Fame Library.
5. Branch Rickey quoted in *Sporting News*, June 21, 1950, 15.
6. *Sporting Life*, September 16, 1921, 11.
7. Ty Cobb file, National Baseball Hall of Fame Library.
8. McCallum, *The Tiger Wore Spikes*, 79.
9. *New York Times*, January 17, 1912, 44.
10. *Philadelphia Public Ledger*, May 16, 1912, 8.
11. *Sporting Life*, May 25, 1912, 4.
12. Cobb, with Stump, *My Life in Baseball*, 43.
13. Ty Cobb file, National Baseball Hall of Fame Library.
14. *Sporting Life*, June 10, 1912, 7.

15. *Philadelphia Public Ledger*, May 18, 1912, 7.
16. Ernie Harwell Collection files, Burton Historical Collection, Detroit Public Library.
17. Cobb, *My Life in Baseball*, 140.
18. Donald M. Honig, *Baseball When the Grass Was Real*, 40.
19. *Sporting News*, May 1, 1913, 1.
20. *New York Times*, April 21, 1913, 12.
21. Cobb, with Stump, *My Life in Baseball*, vi.
22. *Sporting News*, June 21, 1950, 15.
23. Ibid.
24. Ty Cobb file, National Baseball Hall of Fame Library.
25. Ibid.

Ty Cobb in his U.S. Army captain's uniform in 1917. © *Bettmann/CORBIS*.

WAR AND THE LIVELY BALL

In the spring of 1917, Ty Cobb was just 30 years old despite being a veteran of twelve seasons in the big leagues. That experience was ammunition in Cobb's arsenal, as he took note of every player in the league and recognized their weaknesses. Cobb had most of the league terrified of him, and he exploited that advantage. "Every great batter works on the theory that the pitcher is more afraid of him than he is of the pitcher."[1] A student of hitting, which he considered a scientific matter, Cobb had developed an encyclopedic knowledge of the pitchers in the league. "Every opposing pitcher is a special problem. You learn to know them, all their mental peculiarities, what they're likely to do under certain circumstances. . . . You learn their mental quirks and preferences. You catalogue them in your brain, and have them ready, for instant use, when you need them."[2]

On March 31, in Dallas for an exhibition series against the National League's New York Giants, Cobb got himself embroiled in a feud that ended with the Georgia Peach threatening to kill Giants manager John McGraw. New York shortstop Art Fletcher recalled years later: "Cobb was late arriving at the park. He had been out at the country club playing golf. That in itself would have been enough to get us on him."[3] McGraw and his team razzed Cobb as he strolled in late for their exhibition game, and when Cobb insisted on taking a few practice cuts that delayed the start even longer, the Giants were steaming. After he singled early in the game, Cobb slid hard into Charles "Buck" Herzog, tearing the second baseman's trousers. Some pushing and shoving ensued, with Cobb earning an ejection from home plate umpire Bill Brennan, who happened to be a personal friend of McGraw's. That evening in the players' hotel, which housed both the Tigers and the Giants, Herzog, still seething from the hard slide, challenged Cobb to a fight. Within minutes, members of both teams were jammed into Ty's room, furniture had been moved, and a makeshift boxing arena had formed. Adhering to gentleman's rules, Cobb and Herzog each chose a second for their fight, Herzog picking friend Heinie Zimmerman, the Giants third baseman, and Cobb selecting Oscar Stanage. Longtime Detroit equipment manager Harry Tuthill was agreed upon as the referee. Cobb and Herzog fought for several minutes as their teammates watched from the sidelines. Accounts differ as to the severity of the beating, but most agree that Cobb whipped Herzog, pinning him down with his superior size and pounding him with blows from both fists before Tuthill stopped the fracas. In his room later, Herzog was bruised, but proud of his fight with Cobb. "I got the hell kicked out of me, but I knocked the bum down and you know that swell-head will never get over the fact that a little guy like me had him on the floor."[4] As far as Cobb and Herzog were concerned, that was the end of the conflict, but the next morning McGraw started it up again. As Cobb passed through the lobby, McGraw confronted the Tigers star and gave him a tongue-lashing. Cobb, who towered over McGraw by nearly five inches, told the Giants manager that he would kill him if he ever spoke to him that way again.

With the battle lines drawn between Cobb and McGraw, the Tigers gave Ty permission to abandon the exhibition tour and meet the team in Detroit for the start of the season. On April 2, news of a much larger battle grabbed headlines—the United States had finally declared war on Germany and was entering the war in Europe. On April 9, Cobb rejoined his team in Toledo, Ohio, for an exhibition game.

When the 1917 regular season opened in mid-April, baseball was in a patriotic mood. In New York, former Tiger pitcher Wild Bill Donovan, now managing the Yankees, marched his team onto the field for a pregame ceremony. Carrying bats on their shoulders as if they were rifles, the players marched in formation and presented the colors to Major General Leonard Wood of the U.S. Army, who later threw out the first pitch. In both leagues, teams began drilling as if they were military units, with the Tigers taking up the practice a few days into the season. Each major league team was assigned a drill instructor, and when Detroit's instructor (a Sergeant Thorne) was called to active duty, second baseman Ralph Young, who had graduated from a military academy, took over.

Unlike the Second World War, where the U.S. entered the conflict during baseball's off-season and players voluntarily entered the service, America did not begin to call up citizens for duty until a few months after declaring war in 1917. Major league ballplayers, for the most part, did not enter military service during the 1917 season. Therefore, outside of the military drilling, the regular season was barely affected by the overseas conflict.

The Tigers opened the season at home on April 11, losing to the Indians 6–4. By the end of the month the team was wallowing in seventh. Cobb was hitting .320, a decent mark, but below his standards. It was the pitching staff that was to blame for the slow start. Ehmke and Coveleski, especially, had gotten off to a rough start.

In June, Cobb carried the team on his back to a 17–10 record, moving the club over the .500 mark and into fourth place. That month, Cobb hit a blistering .459 (51 for 111) with 9 doubles, 8 triples, 3 home runs, and 12 stolen bases. Cobb punctuated his month of success on June 30 in St. Louis. After a pair of hits in the opener of a double-header, Cobb belted a mammoth home run over the right field stands in the second contest, prompting "the most spontaneous and prolonged applause that has ever greeted an alien enemy athlete."[5]

From May 31 to July 5, Cobb hit in thirty-five consecutive games, the second longest streak of his career. During the streak, Cobb enjoyed a 5-for-5 game against the Yankees in New York on June 5, which began an amazing streak of eight straight games with two or more hits. In July, Cobb continued his barrage of hits, exploding for two four-hit games and a five-hit game in one week. At the end of July, Cobb was leading the league with a .388 batting average, but Detroit was a distant eight and one-half games out of first place.

In August, the Tigers skidded farther back in the standings, but Cobb maintained his batting lead and pushed his average closer to .400 by month's end. On August 25, at Navin Field, the Tigers held Sam Crawford Day, attracting a sizable crowd despite the unseasonably cool temperatures of that late summer. Earlier in the season, Hughie Jennings had left Crawford behind in Detroit as the team traveled east for a road trip. At age 37, Crawford's best seasons were behind him. He'd sunk to a .286 mark the previous season, and was languishing below .200 when Jennings benched him in favor of Harry Heilmann. On his special day, Jennings inserted Wahoo Sam in right field. In the fifth inning, Crawford thrilled the crowd by launching a deep fly to right field, but Philadelphia outfielder Charlie Jamieson spoiled the moment when he reached up and stole a home run from Sam. The Tigers went on to win the game 4–2. A few weeks later, just prior to Detroit's departure on their final road trip, Crawford made his last appearance in the big leagues, failing as a pinch hitter. His 19-year career was over, with a record 312 triples to his credit, in addition to a .309 batting average and more than 2,900 hits. A quiet, durable player, Crawford had also set the record for most consecutive games, having played 472 straight games for Detroit from 1908 to 1911. While his teammates were wrapping up their 1917 season with an eastern swing, Crawford returned to his California home.

The next season, Crawford began a four-year career as an umpire in the Pacific Coast League.

Cobb finished the season by batting safely in his last thirteen games, helping Detroit to nine wins during that span. His final average stood at .383, good enough for his tenth batting title. Avenging his defeat in the 1916 batting race, Ty had won the title by a whopping thirty-one points over Tris Speaker. Cobb had recorded his third consecutive 200-hit season and seventh in his career, having banged out 225 in total. He had scored 107 runs and approached his career-highs with 44 doubles and 23 triples, both of which led the loop. He also paced the league with 55 stolen bases. It was the sixth and final time he would lead the league in that category. With another batting title and a thirty-five-game hitting streak to his credit, Cobb had been the most dangerous player in the league once again.

In the off-season, Cobb signed a contract for the 1918 season for the sum of $20,000, the same figure he had earned in 1917. Cobb also applied to the Augusta Draft Board, making himself eligible for military service. At 31 years of age, Cobb was placed in a special class. The military would draft younger men before turning to Cobb's group.

The war in Europe dominated headlines in 1918. In March, as the Germans were launching the first of five major offensives to win the war before U.S. troops could swing the outcome, the Tigers reported to Waxahachie for spring training. Cobb once again reported late, preferring to join the club later that month in Dallas for an exhibition series. During the spring, Cobb came down with the flu, which kept him out of the Detroit line-up for Opening Day at Cleveland.

Hampered by injuries and the loss of pitchers Willie Mitchell and Howard Ehmke to military service, the Tigers played terribly in the opening months of 1918. In April, when many games were rained out, the team won two games and lost four. In May, the Tigers suffered through a seven-game losing streak out east against New York, Boston, and Philadelphia. Cobb's performance was inconsistent in the early going, and when he hurt his shoulder in Washington on May 25, he was out of the line-up. The injury, which Cobb sustained when he dove in the outfield to make a dazzling catch, had a lasting impact. Cobb's throwing arm, which had once been very strong, was never quite the same. Later in the 1918 season, Cobb hurt his nonthrowing shoulder twice in the same game.

On August 14, Cobb and the Tigers began a three-game series against the Senators in the nation's capital. While there, Cobb visited the War Department, where he took his mandatory army physical and applied for the Chemical Warfare Service. Because he was 31 years old, Cobb was placed in a special draft category and most likely wouldn't have been called to duty. But Cobb, spurred by the memory of Thomas Reade Roots Cobb, the Civil War hero, felt compelled to get into the fight. A few days later, while Detroit was in New York to play the Yankees, Cobb received word that he had been accepted into the Chemical Warfare Service. He was to report in October.

The Chemical Warfare Service (CWS) had been organized by General John J. Pershing in response to several deadly poison gas attacks on American troops by the Germans. The attacks had generated considerable outrage, and the creation of the CWS was front-page news. The CWS was created to perfect methods to withstand poison gas attacks, but more importantly (and controversially), it was also charged with developing poisononous gas weapons to be used against the Germans in Europe. Other baseball figures who would also serve in the CWS included Christy Mathewson, Branch Rickey, and George Sisler.[6]

But prior to reporting to the CWS, Cobb had a regular season to finish. After a slow start, he'd caught fire in May and June and once again led the batting race. In July, he strung together a twenty-game hitting streak, batting .568 during the run. With America entering the war, 1918 was a difficult season for major league baseball, as attendance dipped considerably. In midsummer, league officials, supported by the War Department, decided to shorten the season by a month. In keeping with the "work or fight" philosophy, the baseball season would end on Labor Day, after which the World Series would be played.

The country was understandably indifferent to the national pastime as teams wrapped up their schedules. The Tigers struggled to a 55–71 record, which left them in seventh place, their worst showing since 1904. On September 1, during a meaningless double-header against the Browns in St. Louis, Cobb made his first appearance as a pitcher at the big-league level. In the second game, Cobb relieved George Cunningham and pitched two innings of one-run ball. He surrendered three hits, including one to Browns first baseman George Sisler, who also pitched in the game. The next day, back in Detroit against the White Sox, Cobb pitched in relief with identical results—two innings, three hits, and one earned run allowed. The stints on the mound did little to interrupt Cobb's batting feats; he went 15 for 24 in the last five games of the season. His batting exploits had landed him another batting title, his eleventh. His final mark was .382, almost exactly his figure from the previous year. In the abbreviated season, Cobb had played 111 games, collected 161 hits and stolen 34 bases.

With the season over and war raging in Europe, no one knew when baseball would resume. While preparing to report to the CWS, Cobb hinted that he was through with the game. Nearing his thirty-second birthday, and with the war dragging on in France, he felt it was possible that he would never step on a ballfield again.

After a few weeks in Augusta with Charlotte and his children, Ty arrived in New York and reported for duty on October 1. He was commissioned as a captain in the U.S. Army, and after a relatively short time in accelerated training, he and his unit sailed for France. The Army hoped that Cobb and the other sports figures in the CWS would be effective in training enlisted men in the area of chemical and biological warfare. But according to Cobb, he ended up training "the darnedest bunch of culls the World War I Army ever grouped in one outfit."[7]

The training exercises, though they took place far behind the front lines, were extremely dangerous. Cobb would march his troops into an airtight chamber, where they were to quickly assemble their gas masks when they received a signal that the poison was about to filter into the room. On one occasion, Cobb and his troops either missed or were slow to react to the signal, and many of them stumbled from the chamber having inhaled the poison into their lungs. For weeks Cobb suffered with a hacking cough while a "colorless discharge" drained from his chest. Others were not so lucky—they died after the exposure. Christy Mathewson, the great National League hurler who also served as an officer in the CWS, inhaled so much of the gas while in France that he later developed tuberculosis. He died from the disease seven years later, in 1925.

Cobb had been in France less than a month when the war ended suddenly on November 11. The Allies, bolstered by the influx of American troops, had deflected the last German offensives and hurtled the aggressors back into the Rhine. When the Hindenberg Line was breached by the Allies, the Germans collapsed in disarray. Within a few weeks, Cobb was onboard the largest ship in the world, the U.S.S. *Leviathan*, one of the first transport ships back to the United States. Cornered by newsmen in New York upon his arrival, Cobb continued to insist he was through with baseball, despite the early demise of his military career. He spent the rest of 1918 and the first few months of 1919 near Augusta, spending time with his family and hunting with friends.

When the time for spring training arrived, Cobb caught the itch to play baseball once again. Because his contract with the Tigers had expired, Cobb was an unsigned player. He soon began making salary demands, even sending a telegram to sportswriters in Detroit complaining that Frank Navin had neglected to send him an offer. During the month of March, while Tiger players trained in Macon, Georgia, only a short distance from Ty's front door, Cobb and Navin engaged in another bitter salary dispute, played out as usual in the newspapers. Navin eventually sent Cobb an offer for 1919, which called for the batting champion to accept a reduction in salary. Navin explained that due to the war-torn season of 1918, which caused great losses to the owners, cuts were necessary. Predictably, Cobb didn't expect the policy to extend to him. Eventually, Navin offered $20,000, the same salary Ty had earned in 1918, and Cobb accepted.

When the season began on April 25 in Detroit, Cobb went 2 for 4 with a double, helping Howard Ehmke to a 4–2 victory over the Indians. Navin and Jennings had high hopes for the 1919 season, having retooled the club. In January, Navin had traded Ossie Vitt, the team's longtime third baseman, to the Red Sox for catcher Eddie Ainsmith, reserve outfielder Charles "Chick" Shorten, and a freakish six-foot, seven-inch pitcher with the unfortunate name of "Slim" Love. The team had also purchased Dutch Leonard, a veteran left-handed pitcher, with whom Cobb had quarreled when Leonard had been with the Red Sox. To Cobb's left in the Tigers outfield was newcomer Ira Flagstead, a hard-hitting rookie from Montague, Michigan.

Despite the heightened expectations of Tiger brass, the team stumbled in the early going, losing fourteen of their first nineteen games. Then, after a 12–2 stretch, the Bengals were over the .500 mark and just six games behind the White Sox. At the end of May, Cobb was in his customary spot at the top of the American League batting race, thanks in part to a 14 for 27 stretch against Boston and Philadelphia pitching.

In the middle of June, Cobb suffered a painful injury to his leg and missed nearly three weeks of action. When he returned in Chicago for the usual Independence Day double-header, the Tigers dropped a pair of games to the White Sox, dropping them eight and one-half games back of the upstart Yankees, who had slipped into first place. But Cobb's return to the line-up paid dividends later that month, as the team went on an 18–5 tear. On July 20, in an 8–0 victory over the Red Sox, Cobb slapped two hits, including a double. The next day he collected three hits and stole a base against Babe Ruth, and he followed with two more hits the next day in a 2–1 win. Later, on July 30, in the second game of a twin bill at Fenway Park in Boston, Cobb went 4 for 4 as he started a 14 for 21 hot streak.

Hitting at a feverish clip, Cobb once again drove the team to success, as Detroit won fourteen of sixteen games in August. Cobb cemented his hold on the batting lead, hitting .449 during the month of August with 48 hits, including 9 doubles, 3 triples, and 1 home run. Along with Veach and Flagstead, who were both batting over .350 for the season, the Tigers had the most potent outfield attack in the game. On August 25, in a crucial game against their Boston rivals, Cobb nearly completed a dramatic comeback win with his daring running. Trailing 5–2 in the bottom of the ninth inning, Detroit scratched across a run to draw closer. With a man on base, Cobb then hit a deep shot to left center that bounced to the outfield wall, scoring the Tigers fourth run. Representing the tying run, Cobb raced around the bases, sprinting around third only to find the ball waiting for him at home. He was tagged for the final out of the game as Detroit lost 5–4.

When Detroit entered a double-header against the first place White Sox on Labor Day, they had faint hopes of getting into the race. But after the Sox swept the Tigers by the scores of 6–0 and 5–1, those hopes were destroyed. But there was much left to play for. Unlike in previous years when the top four teams in the league shared postseason money, only the top three would get such a bonus in 1919. Entering a three-game set in New York on September 19, Detroit was two and one-half games ahead of the Yankees for third place. But with Cobb going 1 for 4, the Bengals were defeated 7–0, and the next day the Yankees won again, 6–3. After losing the finale by the score of 4–3, Detroit sunk to fourth place—"out of the money" in the standings. The Tigers then reeled off five straight victories to finish the season, with Cobb putting an exclamation point on his season with three hits in the finale. Unfortunately, the Yankees won a make-up game the next day and slipped into third place. It cost each member of the Tiger team roughly $550.

Cobb, who in the spring had been unsure if he wanted to play baseball at all, had won another batting championship, the twelfth of his career. In the truncated 140-game schedule, Cobb had banged out a league-high 191 hits and swiped 28 bases, the second-leading figure in the AL. Oddly, he managed to hit just one home run for the season, his lowest output since 1906, but his batting mark of .384 showed how consistent he had become—he had hit .382 and .383 the previous two seasons.

The Tigers third-place finish had been an improvement, but once again baseball's best player was not going to the World Series. At nearly 33 years old, Cobb was unsure if he'd ever get a chance to win the one trophy that had eluded his grasp—a world championship.

As usual, the one great weakness of the Detroit Tigers in 1919 had been pitching. The offense had placed third in the American League with 618 runs, led by the production of Cobb, Veach, Flagstead, and Heilmann. But the pitching staff's ERA of 3.30 was sixth out of the eight AL teams. Bobby Veach, the fine left fielder, had enjoyed his finest season in the big leagues, finishing as runner-up to Cobb in the batting race at .355, and driving in 101 runs. Veach was a sleek but powerful slugger from Kentucky, who spent his career overshadowed by Cobb, Sam Crawford, and later, Harry Heilmann. He batted .310 in a 14-year career that stretched to 1925.

That fall, as baseball debated the validity of the World Series between the White Sox and Cincinnati, which seemed a bit fishy to most observers, Cobb was home getting acquainted with his new daughter Beverly. The 1919 World

Series was surrounded by the influence of gamblers, who approached both the White Sox and Reds to throw games. A contingent of White Sox players, led by first baseman Arnold "Chick" Gandil and Eddie Cicotte, conspired to throw the Series. Ultimately, eight Chicago players were banned from baseball for their part in the scandal. In November, Cobb signed another one-year contract with the Tigers, accepting Navin's proposal of $20,000, the same figure he'd earned for 1919. After a winter of hunting, Ty rejoined the Tigers for an exhibition game in March of 1920 in Indianapolis.

Hughie Jennings, who had penned his name to another one-year deal to manage the Tigers, had an explosive offensive team, but another suspect pitching corps. The club arrived in Chicago on April 12 and opened their season two days later against the White Sox. With gambling conspiracies and rumors swirling around the Chicago club, 1920 would prove to be a nightmare for Sox manager William "Kid" Gleason.

On Opening Day, Hooks Dauss, a 21-game winner the year before, lost a tough game to Claude "Lefty" Williams 3–2. Detroit native Eddie Cicotte, who had played with Cobb in Augusta in 1905, shut the Tigers out the following day 4–0. When Yancy "Doc" Ayers, who had been acquired the previous season from Washington, was shelled the next day 11–4, Detroit was on their way to the worst start in franchise history.

Cobb collected hits in each of the first four games of the season, but then dipped into the longest hitless skid of his career. For five consecutive games Cobb was held without a hit, as he went 0 for 17 and saw his batting average drop to .176. As Cobb struggled, the team scored a total of five runs in a six-game stretch, running their record to 0–11. On May 1, Cleveland pummeled Howard Ehmke 9–3, and when Jim Bagby defeated the Tigers 5–2 the next afternoon, Detroit had set a major league record for most losses to start a season with thirteen.

As the Tigers sunk to historic depths, Jennings quickly lost grasp of his players. During the course of the season, Heilmann, Ira Flagstead, Ehmke, and Dutch Leonard openly challenged the skipper. Jennings responded by benching Heilmann and Flagstead for short stretches, while Leonard eventually quit the club in September, returning to his home on the West Coast. With Cobb and shortstop Donie Bush the only players remaining from Jennings' pennant-winning days, the manager gradually became isolated, with even the Detroit media turning on him. In Cleveland, Tris Speaker was enjoying success as player-manager of the Indians, which led to speculation that Cobb would also assume that role.

But despite a personal distrust of Jennings and contempt for the manager's drinking problems, Cobb publicly supported the Tigers skipper. On the diamond, Cobb rebounded from his difficult start and began hitting like the Cobb of old. Beginning on May 7, he began a stretch where he hit in thirty-three of thirty-five games, raising his batting average more than 150 points in the process. For most of the season Detroit rested in seventh place, spared the disgrace of the cellar only because Connie Mack once again had a miserable group of players in Philadelphia. Meanwhile, the White Sox, Indians, and Yankees (led by Babe Ruth, whom New York had purchased from Boston in the off-season) engaged in a three-team tug-o-war for first place.

In early June, just as he was getting hot with the bat, Cobb suffered the worst injury of his playing career. As he chased a fly ball in right center in Chicago's Comiskey Park, he collided with Flagstead and fell to the ground in pain. He had wrenched his left knee, tearing ligaments. After consulting a specialist in Chicago, Cobb was sent home to Augusta to recuperate.[8]

He was out of the line-up for more than a month, not returning until July 8, when he delivered a dramatic ninth-inning, game-tying single against the Yankees. With Bobby Veach on third representing the winning run, he and Cobb attempted a double steal. Despite his still-aching knee, Cobb hustled safely into second base as Veach scored on a bad throw to give the Tigers the victory. Two days later, Cobb was back in the line-up for good, starting a twenty-game hitting streak in which he batted .471.

But despite his heroic batting feats, Cobb's knee was far from healed. On several occasions the rest of the season, Cobb reinjured the leg, though he stubbornly refused to miss many more games. In August, he suffered through a 4 for 34 stretch but still remained at his station in center field.

While many of his teammates were going through the motions, Cobb tried valiantly to get back in the batting race. But George Sisler, the popular Browns' first baseman, would not relent. Most of the summer, the left-handed Sisler kept his average well over the .400 mark, and with few games remaining to close the gap, Cobb had no chance. Sisler would end the campaign with a .407 average, more than seventy points higher than Cobb.

On August 16, at the Polo Grounds in New York, baseball was shocked when Cleveland shortstop Ray Chapman died after being struck in the left temple by a pitched ball from Carl Mays. It was the first on-field fatality in major league history. Newspapers tried to get Cobb's reaction to the beaning, but no evidence exists that he ever responded on the record. Mays had been a thorn in Cobb's side dating back to his days with the Red Sox. A few New York papers erroneously reported that Cobb had called for Mays to be suspended for life, which served to rile Yankee fans. When the Tigers opened a four-game match with the Yankees in New York on August 21, Cobb received a chorus of boos and a few death threats.

The circus atmosphere was one more stress that Cobb had to deal with in 1920, in addition to the constant losing and his own injuries. Rising to the occasion, Cobb had one of the most triumphant days of his career on August 22, when he lashed out five hits and drove in two runs to help Detroit defeat the Yanks 11–9. As more than 32,000 fans called for his scalp, Cobb continued his barrage the next afternoon against Mays, who was making his first start since the Chapman beaning. Ty collected two hits as Detroit lost 10–0. But Cobb had the last laugh, as the Tigers won the finale of the series, thus taking three of four and hurting the Yankees' pennant chances.

In September, Cobb made his usual late-season rush, as the baseball world buzzed over the Chapman incident and the gambling scandal that hung like a black cloud over the White Sox. Despite his nagging knee, Cobb grabbed his hits in bunches, banging out thirteen multi-hit games during September. In mid-September, in a series against New York, Cobb crossed paths with Yankees rookie catcher Fred "Bootnose" Hofmann, who was just up from the minor leagues. In the first game of the series, as Cobb entered the batter's box, Hofmann sneered, "So this is the great 'Georgia Peach'?" Cobb, surprised at the young catcher's audacity, growled back, "Busher, I'm going to get on base, and when I do, I'm coming around." After lining a single, Cobb stole second and then attempted to score on a deep grounder to the shortstop. The shortstop's throw had Cobb beat by a large margin, as Hofmann waited with delight to apply a hard tag. But just as Hofmann attempted to slap the tag on Cobb, Ty flung himself through the air feet-first and tore into the unsuspecting catcher. Cobb's sharpened spikes found their mark, ripping Hofmann's chest protector and tearing into the catcher's leg. Cobb, Hofmann, and the ball all went to the ground in separate directions. Cobb then picked himself up, stepped over the dazed Hofmann, dusted dirt into the catcher's face, and sneered, "Yes, you fresh busher, that was the great 'Georgia Peach.'" It was a story that Hofmann spun the rest of his life.[9]

On September 27, in Chicago, where the Tigers had opened their disastrous season, and Cobb had suffered his knee injury, most of the infamous "Black Sox" coconspirators played their final major league game. Chicago right-hander Dickie Kerr baffled the Tigers 2–0, as Joe Jackson, George "Buck" Weaver, Oscar "Happy" Felsch, Arnold "Chick" Gandil, Charles "Swede" Risberg, and Fred McMullin played big-league baseball for the last time. Those six, along with pitchers Eddie Cicotte and Lefty Williams, were indicted the next day for accepting bribes to throw the 1919 World Series. In the short term it spelled the end of the White Sox hopes for a pennant in 1920, as they fell two games short of Tris Speaker's Indians. But in the long term it created a scandal that rocked the baseball world and led to the creation of the office of the commissioner. Jackson, whom Cobb had once called, "the finest natural hitter in the history of the game,"[10] had thrown away a chance to become one of the greatest players in baseball history.

Cobb's knee injury had limited him to 112 games, in which he batted .334, his lowest mark since the 1908 season. With Babe Ruth dominating the headlines with his mighty home-run blasts, Cobb's day seemed to be over. Increasingly, players were holding the bat at the end of the handle and swinging as hard as they could, the method utilized by the Babe. In an interview after the season, Cobb warned that Ruth would have a difficult time building on his success:

> The big guy is a wonder, but he has a big job ahead of him to keep place in the public's eye that he now holds. Hitting home runs day after day is far more difficult than doing the things I have done to keep my name before the public. My task is to make base hits and show some speed on the bases. Ruth's task is to keep hitting the ball further than anyone else can. In order to continue doing that, Ruth must take the best care of himself. There must be coordination between the eye and the muscles of the body. He must be able to time the ball perfectly. If Ruth takes on weight, increases his waistline, his natural swing is certain to suffer. His eye won't be right. I am afraid Ruth is going to get heavy. If he does, the pitchers will soon gain the mastery over him. When they do he is going to slip rapidly. Ruth must be a well-conditioned athlete or his fame is going to be short-lived.[11]

In 1920, home run totals and runs scored increased at nearly historic proportions, prompting scribes to write about the "lively ball." Speculation arose that Organized Baseball had tinkered with the baseball to make it more lively following the 1918–1919 seasons, when attendance dipped. But, actually, attendance had rebounded in 1919, and runs-scored totals were up that season as well. Ruth had belted 29 homers in 1919 in a 140-game schedule. In 1920 he swatted 54, which was quite an increase, but not outside the realm of natural progression. No evidence existed that officials had tampered with the baseball prior to the 1920 season.

A more logical explanation for the increase in runs and homers did present itself. With Ruth as an example, batters began to swing for the fences. The league also began to crack down on the use of dirty and stained baseballs. In the past, an entire game could be played with one or two baseballs, but starting after World War I, teams began to allow fans to keep the balls that entered the stands, forcing the introduction of new baseballs into play. Pitchers no longer had a dark, soiled, often wet sphere to hurl toward the plate. Batters could see the ball better, and with their new home-run strategy, they took advantage. Within a few years, players in both leagues would be slugging homers at Ruthian rates. A few players avoided the hysteria and continued to play baseball one base at a time, relying on their wits. Cobb was chief among them.

The 1920 Detroit Tigers had finished an embarrassing seventh in the AL standings, losing ninety-three games. Frank Navin, now one of the controlling owners of the team after W. H. Yawkey's death, was not pleased. After fourteen seasons at the helm, Hughie Jennings was fired. The enthusiastic Jennings, who had become a fan favorite with his trademark "Eeyah" shouts of encouragement from the coaches' box, had lost control of the team.

Almost immediately, Cobb's name was at the top of the list to replace Jennings. Also under consideration was George Stallings, who had managed the Boston Braves to their stunning 1914 World Series upset over the Athletics. But Stallings, who like Bill Armour, Cobb's first major league manager, wore a suit in the dugout, hadn't had a winning season in Boston for several years. Clarence "Pants" Rowland, who had lost his managerial job with the White Sox two years earlier despite having won the 1917 World Series, was also a frontrunner. But Cobb, like most ballplayers in the league, felt that Rowland was a "bush league manager,"[12] and wanted no part of him.

Navin eventually offered the job to Cobb, but Ty was reluctant to accept the position. In December, with the vacancy still unfilled, sportswriter E. A. Batchelor entered the negotiations. As a personal friend of Cobb, Batchelor didn't want to see Rowland or anyone else get the Detroit job. He felt that Cobb could be as successful as Tris Speaker in Cleveland, who had just led his club to the World Championship. After some prodding from Batchelor, Cobb met with Navin in New York on December 18—Ty's thirty-fourth birthday—and accepted the position. Navin agreed to pay Cobb $35,000 to both play for and manage the club, a figure Cobb was delighted to accept; it made him the highest paid player in the game.

Yet despite the financial reward, Cobb was still unsure of his decision. New York writer Damon Runyon commented that the deal was "quite a birthday present." But Cobb responded later to Runyon off the record, telling him it was "anything but a present."[13] Ty Cobb, a twelve-time batting champion, was about to begin a second career as a manager.

NOTES

1. McCallum, *The Tiger Wore Spikes*, 122.
2. *Baseball Magazine*, January 1927, 340.

3. Joseph Durso, *Casey and Mr. McGraw* (St. Louis: The Sporting News, 1989), 89.

4. Ibid.

5. Charles C. Alexander, *Ty Cobb*, 163.

6. Charles E. Heller, *Chemical Warfare in World War I: The American Experience 1917–1918* (Washington, DC: Government Printing Office, 1985), 212.

7. Cobb, with Stump, *My Life in Baseball*, 131.

8. McCallum, *The Tiger Wore Spikes*, 122.

9. Bob Broeg, *Superstars of Baseball* (South Bend, IN: Diamond Communications, 1994), 49.

10. Cobb, with Stump, *My Life in Baseball*, 59.

11. *Baseball Magazine*, November 1920, 410.

12. Cobb, with Stump, *My Life in Baseball*, 140.

13. Ty Cobb file, National Baseball Hall of Fame Library.

MANAGING THE TIGERS

It didn't take long for manager Ty Cobb to shake things up on the 1921 Detroit Tigers. In spring training at San Antonio, Texas, Cobb stood the team rules on their head. Where Jennings had insisted on strenuous workouts and long strategy sessions, Cobb backed off his players, giving them more time off. While his players enjoyed the leisurely pace, Cobb worked on his own body, as he tried to shed a few extra pounds he'd acquired in the off-season.

When the team did train, there was an emphasis on the "inside game" of base running and bunting. Cobb desired a team in his own image. He wanted players who could steal a base and move the runner over. He also demanded an end to the cordial relationships many of his players had fostered with members of the New York Giants, who were also training in San Antonio. Cobb felt strongly that fraternization with enemy players made a ballclub soft.

On April 14, the Tigers played their first game under Cobb's tutelage. At home against the White Sox, the Tigers rallied from a four-run deficit, as Cobb used two pinch hitters, a pinch runner, and a relief pitcher to perfection. He also provided a run-scoring double as the "Cobbmen" won 6–5. A brief rough stretch followed, and then the team won seven of eight games in late April and early May, scoring runs in bunches. In a sweep of the White Sox in early May, Detroit outscored Chicago 24–9. The next two days they pounded the Browns by scores of 9–0 and 11–7. The offense was performing wonderfully, with Harry Heilmann off to a great start. Cobb was also getting production from Lu Blue, a switch-hitting rookie first baseman whom Ty had taken under his wing. Up and down the Tiger line-up the batting averages were gaudy: Heilmann was on his way to his first of four batting titles, Cobb, Bobby Veach, third baseman Bob "Ducky" Jones, Blue, catchers Johnny Bassler and Larry Woodall, and reserve outfielder Ira Flagstead, all hit .300 in Cobb's first season at the helm.

The runs kept coming in droves: on May 15 against the Nationals at Navin Field, the Tigers won a 13–10 slugfest. The following afternoon, Cobb had four hits, including a double and a triple, as his team erupted for 17 runs. In all, the Tigers tallied at least 10 runs in 24 different games in 1921. The team would set a major league record with a .316 batting average. Cobb knew how to teach hitting.

But the pitching staff was far less impressive. The team surrendered nearly as many runs as it scored, allowing more than five and one-half runs per nine innings. Only lefty Dutch Leonard had a respectable season, posting a 3.75 ERA in thirty-six games. The rest of the staff was mediocre. At the end of May, Detroit owned a 24–22 record and was sitting in third place. But in June, despite Cobb's .363 average, the Tigers slipped to fifth place. On June 30 in Cleveland, Cobb reinjured his left knee while running the bases. He was out for more than two weeks, and when he returned he used himself sparingly, appearing as a pinch hitter exclusively for a week.

While Cobb's team hit the ball well and still lost, Babe Ruth was leading the New York Yankees with his home-run style of baseball. As a veteran who traced his roots to the dead ball days of the game, Cobb resented Ruth's notoriety. Cobb, a master at bench jockeying, saved special venom for the Yankees slugger, unleashing his tongue in a vicious verbal assault. When he had been with the Red Sox, Ruth had tolerated most of Cobb's insults, but now, as a growing icon in the sport, Ruth was content to butt heads with Cobb. In a series in New York in mid-June, Cobb and Ruth nearly came to blows on several occasions, as Ty bullied the younger Ruth with his taunts. Ruth responded by belting six home runs in the four-game series, which New York swept. In the third contest, the Babe started the game on the mound, earning the win and belting a tape-measure home run. Cobb pounded out seven hits in the series, but left New York vowing to show "that ape" a thing or two the next time.[1]

On July 23, Charlotte Cobb gave birth to a baby boy, James Howell Cobb, the couple's fifth child. In August, Ty rushed to Georgia when his wife became gravelly ill. With his mother and his sister at his side, Cobb spent three days with Charlotte, until her health improved. In his absence, the team suffered a four-game losing streak. In his first game back, against the Yankees at the Polo Grounds, Cobb belted a triple and a home run to halt the losing streak. But August was no different than the rest of the season, as Detroit went 12–17 and fell to sixth place. Cobb's batting average was hovering around the .400 mark, evidence that despite the distractions of managing, he was still able to focus on his own performance.

On August 19, in front of a sparse crowd at Navin Field, Cobb reached a career milestone without fanfare. In the second game of a double-header against the Red Sox, Cobb lined a single off Elmer Myers for the 3,000th hit of his career. At the age of 34, he became the youngest player to ever reach that figure, which was not yet as magical as it would one day become. None of the newspapers of the time mentioned the milestone, and very few would have believed that Cobb—after seventeen seasons in the big leagues—had more than 1,100 hits left in his bat.

While earlier in his career Cobb had been a daredevil on the basepaths, he wasn't foolish, especially in 1921 and later years. Wally Schang, longtime American League catcher, recalled a game between his Yankees and Cobb's Tigers in 1921. With Cobb on third and less than two outs, a fly ball was lifted to medium right field, where Bob Meusel was stationed. Meusel was known to have one of baseball's finest arms, but with Cobb's aggressive nature, Schang figured to have a play at the plate. After the ball rested in Meusel's glove, the right fielder fired a one-hopper to Schang, who peered to his left only to sight Cobb casually standing on third with his hands on his hips. "He knew Meusel's arm and he wasn't about to challenge it."[2]

Even though he was now the team leader and mentor to his players, Cobb still possessed a mean streak. On September 24, Cobb and umpire Billy Evans met in one of baseball's most famous fistfights. With the weight of the season weighing on him and his team languishing in the standings, Cobb was at a breaking point in the game against the Senators in Griffith Stadium. In the fourth inning, he singled and worked his way around to third base. With his old nemesis Walter Johnson on the mound, Cobb tried to steal home. On a close play, Cobb was called out by home plate umpire George Hillebrand. Demonstrating his famous temper, Cobb berated Hillebrand for several minutes. In the fifth inning, Cobb singled again, and on the first pitch he bolted for second base. This time the play was even closer, and when Evans called him out, Cobb was thrown into a rage. As Hillebrand had done the previous inning, Evans deflected Cobb's tirade and refused to eject the Detroit manager.

After the game, Cobb finally got the reaction he'd been seeking, when he barreled into the umpires' dressing room and demanded that Evans fight him. Once both parties agreed that no word of the fight would reach league president Ban Johnson, the two men squared off. In a brawl that one witness described as the "bloodiest he ever saw in baseball,"[3] Cobb and Evans tore into each other for a full ten minutes, with Ty's oldest son, Ty Jr., cheering from the sidelines. Evans, who had boxing experience, was more polished than Cobb, and landed several punches. But Cobb used his edge in size to wrestle the umpire to the ground, where he pounded Evans repeatedly. Finally, Cobb was pulled from Evans and the fight was stopped. Later, the two men shook hands, but the incident was not over.

Home plate umpire Hillebrand, a witness to the melee, felt compelled to report it to the league office. A day later, Commissioner Kenesaw Mountain Landis suspended Cobb as a player for the remainder of the season, though he agreed to allow Ty to manage his team. The decision had cost Cobb a chance to challenge Heilmann for the batting title, with the latter edging his manager by five points. Cobb had played himself in 128 games, overcoming injuries to have his best season in years. He batted .389 with 197 hits, 37 doubles, 16 triples, 101 RBIs, and 22 stolen bases. His 12 home runs were a career high. Despite his disdain for the home-run era, Cobb was starting to hit for more power.

In spite of their record-setting .316 team average, the Tigers had finished twenty-seven games behind of the Yankees in the AL standings, in sixth place. They had improved their win total by ten games in Cobb's first year at the helm, however. The team's real weaknesses had been their pitching and their defense. The Tigers had committed 231 errors, the third highest total in the league. Cobb vowed to field a better fielding team the next season.

In October 1921, Cobb went to California to manage in a four-team instructional league. The primary purpose of the trip was to scout players for the Tigers, who desperately needed pitchers and infielders. Veteran Donie Bush, who had been with Detroit for fourteen seasons, had been dealt to Washington late in the season, creating a hole at shortstop. In addition, Cobb desired a replacement for Ralph Young at second base. When Cobb returned to Georgia in late October, he had convinced Navin to sign two young pitchers from California. In December, the Tigers claimed George Cutshaw, the veteran National League second baseman, on waivers.

With these new additions, Cobb and the Tigers broke camp for spring training in March. Cobb had persuaded Navin to move spring training to Augusta, which allowed the manager to sleep in his own bed. With his team in the bosom of his adopted hometown, Cobb pampered them by hiring two chefs to cook at the team hotel. Once again, as in 1921, Cobb ran a loose camp, preferring afternoon workouts to early morning exercises. After a few weeks of training in Augusta, the team traveled by train to play a series of exhibition games on their way north. In one contest, Cobb tore ligaments in his right ankle and knee, necessitating the use of a cane for the rest of the spring.

By the time the season opened in Cleveland on April 12, Cobb was able to manage a pinch-hitting appearance. It was just the second time since 1907 that he had failed to be in the starting line-up on Opening Day. After missing a few more games with the injury, Cobb was in the line-up for Detroit's home opener on April 20, which Howard Ehmke lost 5–4.

The team once again got off to a poor start, losing their first six games. To add to their misfortune, on April 30, right-hander Charlie Robertson of the White Sox hurled a perfect game against the Tigers in just his third major league start. Less than a week later, on May 5, Cobb faced the embarrassing possibility that his team would be no-hit again. Entering the eighth inning at Navin Field, St. Louis Browns' left-hander Bill Bayne had held the Tigers hitless. Determined to shake up Bayne and scratch across a hit, Cobb ordered five straight pinch hitters, one of whom, reserve catcher Larry Woodall, delivered a single to start the ninth inning. In a rare move, Cobb removed himself for a pinch-hitter: right-handed slugger Bob Fothergill.

In May, Cobb was back from his ankle injury and the Tigers were winning. After taking two of three from the Browns at home, they split with the White Sox before sweeping the Red Sox at Fenway Park in a four-game series. Next up was a series against the Yankees in the Polo Grounds. Spurred by Cobb's hatred of Ruth and the Yankees, the Bengal bats came alive as Detroit won three of four, scoring 30 runs in the series. A New York paper noted that the Tigers were "a peppery, savage and fierce team which took advantage of every opportunity presented—an apt description of Cobb himself."[4]

On May 25, following a 7–3 defeat of Cleveland's Stan Coveleski, Detroit was over the .500 mark for the first time all season. June proved even more exciting for Tiger fans, as Cobb led his club on a 15–3 tear that included an eight-game winning streak in which the offense scored more than 7 runs per contest. Cobb's average was over the .400 mark as he challenged George Sisler for the league lead. Several other Tiger batters were also over the .300 mark, including new shortstop Emory Elmo "Topper" Rigney, a 25-year-old rookie from Texas who was Cobb's latest batting prodigy. Catcher Johnny Bassler, who had hit below .200 before coming to Detroit in 1921, was hitting over .330, while rookie utility infielder Fred Haney, another of Cobb's pupils, was batting over .350 in part-time duty. Bobby Veach, Lu Blue, and Harry Heilmann were also having solid seasons.

On June 24, in Detroit, Cobb's team met the Browns, who were in the rarified position of first place, one and one-half games ahead of the New York Yankees, and two and one-half games ahead of the charging Tigers, who had defeated St. Louis two straight. The Browns were riding the bats of Sisler and their outfield trio of former Tiger Baby Doll Jacobson, Jack Tobin, and Ken Williams. The *St. Louis Post-Dispatch* recorded the odd circumstances of the game, which the Browns won 13–4:

In the sixth inning the lid blew off and 50 policemen were required to quell a most interesting riot at the Browns' dugout. There were numerous contributory causes for the demonstration at the pit. One of them was that the Browns were winning. The immediate cause was the fact that [Browns player-coach] Jimmy Austin threw Lu Blue's first baseman's mitt into the grandstand, not at anyone, particularly, but just to get it away from Haney, the Tiger player who was coaching at first. [Fred Haney, the Tigers rookie utility infielder who would later manage ten seasons in the big leagues, leading the Milwaukee Braves to a World Series title in 1957.] Haney had resorted to tactics designed to disconcert Dave Danforth, who was pitching to Cobb. He [Haney] tossed Blue's glove high into the air every time Dave prepared to deliver a pitch. Austin watched the performance until it chafed and then ran out and grabbed the glove, just as Cobb was swinging wide at a third strike. Jimmy, in his enthusiasm, tossed the glove in the air a la Haney, and it landed in the grandstand. Forthwith fans, ball players and everybody else that cared to, piled into the Browns' dugout, evidently after Austin. Strange to relate Ty Cobb was not in the vanguard of the rioting party. He was busy examining the ball which Danforth had used to strike him out with the bases loaded. . . . It took five minutes for the police to restore order. The umpires couldn't find anything wrong with any player's conduct, so no one was expelled. The game went on, the fans raving more wildly than ever.[5]

The loss was the first of six straight for Detroit, which essentially eliminated them from the race, as they never got to within four games the rest of the way. But Cobb continued to be a terror at the plate. At Boston on July 17, he recorded his fourth five-hit game of the year, setting an American League record. His previous five-hit games came on May 7, July 7, and July 12. The only other player to accomplish that feat had been Willie Keeler.

In August, Heilmann was lost for the season when he broke his collarbone attempting to make a diving catch. But it was the inconsistent pitching that betrayed Cobb. Outside of Herm Pillette, the lanky right-hander whom Cobb had scouted and signed in California during the off-season, no Bengals pitcher was effective. Over the last few weeks of the season, the team was streaky: winning eight of nine, losing six in a row, winning five of six, and ending the year by dropping six of eight. In the final week, Cobb started Pillette three times in a desperate attempt to get the rookie his 20th win, but the rookie had to settle for 19 victories after he lost 4–1 on the penultimate day of the season.

The Browns and Yankees had staged an exciting pennant race, which the Yankees had won for their second straight league title. Cobb finished a distant second to Sisler in the batting race, while Sisler also won the Most Valuable Player Award, which was handed out for the first time since 1914. As a player-manager and previous winner of the award Cobb was ineligible to be considered for the MVP. During his amazing season, Sisler had erased two of Cobb's marks from the AL record book: most hits in a season (257), and longest hitting streak. Sisler had batted in 41 consecutive games during the summer, eclipsing Cobb's 40-gamer from 1911.

Cobb had apparently ended the season with a .401 batting average, having collected 211 hits in 526 official at-bats. But a seemingly routine play back in May left the validity of Cobb's third .400 season in question. The resulting debate raged for years. The controversy stemmed from the game of May 15, when the Tigers were in New York playing the Yankees. The official scorer that day was Jack Kieran, a sportswriter for the *New York Tribune*. There was a steady rain falling when Cobb came to bat late in the game, with many fans having taken cover under the grandstands. The infield was damp and slightly muddy in spots. Cobb bounced a ball toward Yankees shortstop Everett Scott, who came in gingerly on the slippery surface and scooped up the ball. Fred Lieb, who was scoring the game for the Associated Press, later recalled that Scott "had just a little trouble handling the muddy ball." Cobb beat Scott's throw by a full step and Lieb recorded the play as a hit. Kieran recorded it as an error on Scott. Because Kieran's decision was official, at the end of the season there was a discrepancy between the AP's final averages and the official averages released by the league office. This wasn't unusual, but because in this case the scoring decision decided whether or not Cobb had hit .400, it became an issue.

American League President Ban Johnson angered the Baseball Writers Association when he ruled that Lieb's decision would be followed, rather than Kieran's, who was the "official scorer." Lieb would recall with regret that "a decision I made in August 1922 had repercussions for several months and kept popping up years later."[6] Most newspapers criticized Johnson for his decision. A scathing editorial ran in the *New York Monitor*:

> By the grace and goodness of Ban Johnson, President of the American League, Ty Cobb, manager of the Detroit Tigers is a .400 hitter for three years in the big show. According to the official averages at the end of the season, Cobb finished with an average of .3992, having made 210 hits in 526 official times at bat. According to the unofficial averages he finished with an average of .401, having made 211 hits in 526 times at bat. The disputed hit came in a game in New York on May 15. The official scorer decided that Everett Scott had made an error and did not give Cobb a hit. The press associations carried the blow as a "hit" in the scores sent out that day. With-

out asking the official scorer in New York for an explanation or granting him a hearing, Johnson arbitrarily decided that Cobb was entitled to 211 hits and his .400 average. Nobody objects to Ty Cobb, one of the greatest players who ever graced baseball, getting his .400 average, but there is a lot of objection to Johnson deciding hits in Chicago that were made in the Polo Grounds before the eyes of men who know more about the playing end of the game than the Czar of the American League. The next step, not unlikely, is the reversal of some umpire's decision and the awarding of a pennant with the B.B.J. stamp on it.[7]

At first, Cobb responded to the criticism with anger, arguing that New York scorers had been robbing him of hits for years. But within weeks he had cooled off and even joked about the incident with friends in New York at the winter meetings.

Regardless of whether he hit .400 or not, Cobb had enjoyed a banner year. At the age of 35, he collected 211 hits. His leg injuries had hampered his running game—he stole just nine bases—but he still managed 42 doubles and 16 triples. With his performance and the success of his hitting pupils, the Tigers had batted over .300 as a team once again, and climbed into third place in the American League. But if they wanted to contend with the Yankees for league supremacy, the Tigers would have to improve their mound corps.

Despite Cobb's constant nagging of Frank Navin to acquire new arms, the Tigers front office did very little in the off-season. When Cobb reported to spring training in 1923 for his third season as a player-manager, his pitching staff was still very thin. After Hooks Dauss (who had become the winningest pitcher in Detroit history) and Herm Pillette, Cobb had little to work with. One of the few deals that Navin had pulled off was to trade Howard Ehmke (whom Cobb had never liked) to the Red Sox, along with three other players, for veteran second baseman Derrill "Del" Pratt and right-handed pitcher Harry "Rip" Collins. One of three players the Tigers lost in the deal was Floyd "Babe" Herman, a colorful character who was never able to break into the talented Detroit outfield. Several years later, Herman would star for the Brooklyn Dodgers and fashion a .324 lifetime average.

Cobb spent most of spring training working with rookie outfielder Henry "Heinie" Manush, a strong, left-handed batter from Alabama. Manush had tore up the southern leagues much as Cobb had several years earlier. Cobb saw similarities between the 21-year old Manush and himself at a younger age. Within a short time, Cobb had taught Manush how to spray the ball the opposite way. Manush would eventually force himself into the Tigers line-up and carve himself a 17-year career with six different teams, posting a .330 lifetime average. But in 1923, Cobb still began the season with Bobby Veach in left field, and Harry Heilmann in right. The infield was a mix of young and old players, with veterans Pratt and Bob Jones sharing time with youngsters Topper Rigney and Fred Haney. Cobb ran a more traditional training camp in 1923, reinstituting the morning workouts, and increasing the number of running and bunting drills.

Bucking the trend of previous years, Cobb's 1923 team got off to a good start, winning eleven of their first sixteen games to climb atop the standings. Fans were flocking to Navin Field, which had undergone major renovations in the off-season. The park now seated an additional 8,500 fans, who were treated to the exploits of Cobb and his thunderous line-up.

In 1923, a few Tiger players began to wilt under Cobb's managerial style. Playing in center field, Cobb orchestrated games like no other manager in the league, often delaying the action to confer with a fielder or his pitcher. His patience for mistakes was growing thin, and he refused to tolerate a meager effort. "Ty so loved the game of baseball that it was incomprehensible to him that anybody in it ever should do less than his very best, try to make the most of such talent as he had, and work to improve on it."[8]

In mid-June, Cobb quarreled with Bob Jones, and later that month he had words on the bench with Heilmann and Rigney. The team's up-and-down play left them in fourth place, eleven games out, at the end of June. The Yankees were running away with the pennant, and all Detroit could do was fight for what was left. On August 27, Detroit was two games behind Cleveland for second place, but lost ground after being swept by the Browns in St. Louis. Cobb did his best to pitch Dauss, who was having one of his better seasons, as much as possible. Meanwhile, Cobb's relationship with the rest of his pitching staff deteriorated. In September, Cobb and pitcher Ray Francis, who was in his first season with Detroit, fought in the dugout.

In September, the team survived a nightmarish stretch of six double-headers played on six consecutive days, and rallied to fight Cleveland for second place. Spurred by the surprising pitching of rookie left-hander Earl Whitehill from Iowa, and with the regular eight players all healthy for one of the few times all season, Detroit won eleven of their last thirteen games to squeak past the Indians for sole possession of second place. The late-season push had earned each member of the team an extra $1,000 in World Series shares money, the difference between second and third place. The Cobbmen had posted an 83–71 record, their best in four years. But they were still miles from seriously challenging the Yankees for American League bragging rights.

Cobb had used himself more than he had wanted to in 1923, despite suffering from frequent nagging injuries to both of his legs. In 145 games, he batted .340, finishing more than sixty points behind Heilmann, who hit .403 and won his second batting title. During the season, Cobb had become the all-time leader in hits and runs scored, passing Honus Wagner in both cases.

For the third straight season the Tigers had hit .300 as a team. Cobb had found a potent combination in his left-field platoon of Manush and Bob "Fats" Fothergill, a pudgy right-hander with a powerful bat. On the mound, Dauss had won twenty-one games and Pillette had proved adequate, but beyond the success of Whitehill, there was little on the pitching staff to be happy about in 1923.

Yet, the Tigers were doing quite well financially, which pleased Navin. Detroit was booming in the early 1920s, as the automobile industry created thousands of jobs, attracting workers from all over the nation. Helped by the improvements to Navin Field, the Tigers averaged more than 11,000 customers per game. Their season attendance ranked second only to New York, who had moved into Yankee Stadium, their modern new ballpark in the Bronx. Detroit's run scoring machine was a popular draw on the road, and Cobb's frequent antics as manager and player were popular with fans around the league.

The success at the gate and the improvement in the win column ensured Cobb's return for a fourth season as Tiger manager. Navin secured Ty's signature on a contract that called for nearly $40,000 in 1924. In the off-season, Cobb made a hunting trip to Canada and later hunted in Georgia with "Dapper Dan" Howley, a former Tigers coach. Howley had played briefly for the Philadelphia Phillies in 1913 before embarking on a minor league managerial career which led him to Montreal and Toronto of the International League. Hughie Jennings had hired him as a coach in 1919, and Cobb rehired him again in 1921. Despite his reputation for working with pitchers, Howley had little success with the Tigers staff and left to manage in the minors after the 1922 campaign. Howley was known for being impatient and quick tempered, but he got along fairly well with Cobb. The two men became very close friends and frequently hunted together during the 1920s.

In March of 1924, Cobb and his team were back in Augusta for spring training for a third consecutive season. As he had the previous year, Cobb rode his team hard, assigning them to morning workouts and running exercises. When some of his players rebelled against the work load, Cobb was furious. "He made a reputation as a hard task-master in the managerial role but that was largely due to the fact that he had no patience with a player who was satisfied just to get by, rather than putting forth maximum effort."[9] One young player in camp with the Tigers that spring was Charlie Gehringer, a skinny infielder from Fowlerville, Michigan, who had been recruited the previous summer by Bobby Veach. Cobb, despite his rough personality as a manager, was a superb evaluator of hitting talent. After watching Gehringer take batting practice at Navin Field in the fall of 1923, Ty went upstairs in uniform to owner Frank Navin's office and insisted the Tigers sign the youngster. "Cobb took me under his wing right away," Gehringer said, "He kept telling me I was going to be tremendous. He really took care of me the first year or two." In Augusta in 1924, Cobb worked tirelessly with Gehringer. "He more or less told me how to hit, where to stand in the batter's box against certain pitchers, how to spray hit—which I got to be able to do pretty well."[10] But the young left-handed hitter wasn't quite ready for the big league club yet, and Cobb recommended he be shipped to London, Ontario to start the season.

On April 15, 1924, with cautious optimism, the Tigers opened the season at home against Tris Speaker's Indians. Hooks Dauss delighted the hometown crowd, winning 4–3 in front of more than 35,000 fans. With Veach gone, the Tigers now had a starting outfield of Heinie Manush in left, Cobb in center, and Harry Heilmann in right. Bob Fothergill and Al "Red" Wingo, both of whom would enjoy fine seasons at the plate, would provide relief for that trio. Lu Blue was batting leadoff and playing first base, veteran Del Pratt started the season at second base, Topper Rigney was back at short, and the aging Bob Jones was at third base. Cobb's pet, Fred Haney, served as a utility infielder, while Johnny Bassler and Larry Woodall shared the catching chores. Dauss began the season as the team's ace starter, but later gave way to Earl Whitehill.

The Tigers got off to a red-hot start, sweeping the Browns after taking two of three from Cleveland to open the season. On April 26, at home against the rapidly aging White Sox, the Tigers scored 16 runs on 23 hits. With his legs feeling younger than they had in years, Cobb was off to fast start. After he ripped three hits off Ray Kolp of the Browns on May 1, the Georgia Peach was batting a blistering .456 with 26 hits in 14 games.

Cobb used every advantage he could find to get on base. Ted Lyons, the longtime pitcher for the White Sox, recalled that Cobb would "wear a long-sleeve shirt down to his wrists, and if you pitched a ball inside to him, he'd contrive to have it hit that baggy sleeve and he'd get on first base."[11] Against Walter Johnson, the best pitcher in the American League for most of Cobb's career, Ty used an approach that exploited Johnson's nonconfrontational nature. Cobb recognized that "The Big Train" was hesitant to pitch inside, afraid that one of his blazing fastballs would injure an opposing player. In response, Cobb crowded the plate when facing Johnson, which prompted the hurler to pitch Ty away. When Johnson inevitably fell behind in the count, Cobb would step back from the plate and clobber the ball. The result was Cobb's .366 batting average and record 120 hits against Johnson. "I took advantage of Walter's good nature and I hit him better than any man had a right to," Cobb said.[12]

Detroit had won nine of their first twelve games and was in first place, one-half game ahead of the Yankees. In early May the team hit a rough spot, but

Cobb had them back on track at the end of the month. On May 23, Cobb lashed four hits against New York in Yankee Stadium as Detroit captured two of three from the defending World Champions. In that series, the bad blood between Cobb's troops and the Yankees continued. Cobb and Ruth nearly came to blows when Ty heckled the Babe tirelessly. Later, Blue and Haney were involved in a nasty fight with New York first-sacker Wally Pipp.

During one series with the Yankees in 1924, Cobb used his clever mind to embarrass Ruth in front of a huge crowd in Detroit. Jogging in from center field, Cobb pretended to order righty Lil Stoner to intentionally walk Ruth after the hurler had fallen behind three balls to one strike. Hearing this, Ruth relaxed at the plate. On the next pitch, Stoner threw a strike over the meat of the plate, startling Babe and setting Cobb off. Rushing in from his spot in the outfield, Cobb balled out Stoner and replaced him with Ken Holloway. Once again—loudly so that Ruth and the rest of the Yankees heard him clearly—Cobb ordered his pitcher to walk Ruth, threatening a fine if his directive was ignored. Then, Holloway delivered a ball right down the middle for strike three as Ruth stood in the box with the bat on his shoulder. Delighted with his clever ruse, Cobb jogged in from center field, laughing hysterically at the Babe.

The animosity between the two rivals came to a head on June 13. With close to 40,000 fans somehow packed into Navin Field and the surrounding neighborhood, the Tigers and Yankees squared off. With the Yankees on top 10–6 in the ninth inning, Cobb ordered Bert Cole to hit Ruth, who had blasted a pair of home runs in the series already. Cole missed Ruth, but when he drilled Bob Meusel later that inning, both benches cleared. As players from both teams watched in amazement, several thousand fans streamed onto the field, creating a chaotic and dangerous atmosphere. Cobb and Ruth tried to get to each other and throw some punches, but the crowd and a few teammates separated them. Eventually the umpiring crew forfeited the game to the visiting Yankees, as enraged Detroit fans hurled debris at the New York players in their dugout. The next day the two teams concluded their series without incident, but Ban Johnson had fined Ruth fifty dollars, and suspended Cole and Muesel. Somehow, Cobb had escaped punishment. Two days later, Cobb pounded out five hits in a 10–4 laugher over the Red Sox.

Their three losses to New York in early June left the Tigers in third place. Cobb had cooled off, going through a 5-for-26 slump, before a series of multiple-hit performances got him going again. As the summer began, Washington entered the pennant picture, and from that point on it was Detroit, New York, and Washington slugging it out. In July, Detroit ran off an eight-game winning streak, pushing them back into first place, though by a slim margin. In early August, the Tigers split a four-game series against the Yankees in Detroit and then took three of four from the Red Sox, with Cobb stealing home in one of the victories. At one point in August, Cobb strung together a fifteen-game hitting streak, batting .439 with 7 doubles. In one game during the streak, on August 10 against Boston, Cobb displayed his old running form, swiping four bases off pitcher Jack Quinn and catcher Steve O'Neill.[13]

But even though the Tiger pitching staff had improved over previous seasons, there wasn't enough talent on the club to push the team to the top. In August, the team posted a 13–16 record, sinking them five games behind Washington. When the Tigers were swept by the lowly White Sox in a Labor Day doubleheader, their pennant chances were ruined. Even though the Tigers managed a seven-game winning streak in which the offense managed to score an amazing 59 runs, including a 20–1 shellacking of the Indians, the Senators and Yankees were too far ahead. Those two teams battled over the last two weeks of the season, as Cobb pressed his players to keep charging. Detroit did manage to go 17–5 over a stretch near the end of the season, but during that same span Washington was 17–6 and New York was 15–7.

In a crucial series for the Yankees in Detroit, September 19–21, the Tigers stymied their rivals and spoiled their chances at the pennant with a three-game sweep. Cobb was a menace, berating the Yankee hitters from center field on defense, and taunting them from the third base coach's box when his team was on offense. Invigorated at the thought of ruining Ruth's chances at another flag, Cobb went 6 for 13 with 3 runs scored, a double, 2 stolen bases, and 2 RBIs in the sweep. In the finale, he battered Waite Hoyt for three hits as Earl Whitehill defeated the Yankees 4–3. Late in the game, Cobb was nearly attacked by Yankees rookie first baseman Lou Gehrig and shortstop Everett Scott, who were both fed up with Ty's constant baiting.

Detroit finished the season in third place, six games behind Washington, who had captured their first American League pennant. Their 86 wins would be the highest of Ty's six seasons as Tiger manager. Cobb had reached the 200-hit mark for the ninth and final time of his career. His 23 stolen bases were his highest total in five years, since before his leg injuries. He had been more patient at the plate, drawing 85 walks, the second-highest mark of his career. As he had been throughout his career, Cobb was difficult to strike out in 1924, fanning just 18 times. He batted .338 and finished well behind Ruth in the batting race, but at the age of 37, his performance was remarkable. No other player his age had ever been so productive.

Washington won the 1924 World Series, which Cobb attended and covered for a newspaper syndicate. Walter Johnson, the great hurler, had finally earned a World Series title. It was something Cobb dreamed of, but would never achieve.

For the first time in four years, Babe Ruth and the Yankees did not play in the World Series. The slugger accepted a job covering the series for a New York newspaper, a task that perched him next to his bitter enemy Cobb in the press box. Over the course of the Series, Cobb and Ruth made amends. Beginning the next season, the two would enjoy a more friendly relationship, though Cobb continued to resent the attention Ruth received for his home-run feats.[14]

In the winter of 1924–1925, Cobb's off-season activities were typical—hunting and relaxing in Georgia with his family. Early in the spring of 1925, Cobb signed another one-year contract to manage the Tigers for the same salary he had made the previous season: $40,000.

But Cobb's heart was not in managing, and as he grew older, he realized his time in baseball was passing. The days of clawing and scratching for runs was gone. The new player was concerned with one thing—belting home runs. In his opinion, the new brand of baseball was inferior to the style he had employed in his prime. He wished for a return to the attitude of the feisty 1907–1909 pennant-winning Tigers. "Those were the boys, I tell you. They had the stuff. Their type has vanished. You couldn't beat them because they wouldn't let you. If I could only get about six players like them, we would have a winning team."[15]

The 1925 Tigers had little chance of being winners after they put themselves in a hole early in the season. Following a routine spring training camp in Augusta, Cobb led his team north to begin the season against the White Sox in Detroit on April 14. Dutch Leonard, who had returned from retirement, pitched the Tigers to a 4–3 victory. But the Bengals proceeded to lose fourteen of their next eighteen games as they spiraled into the AL cellar. Cobb watched helplessly, as a bad case of the flu limited him to just one pinch-hitting appearance in the first two weeks of the season.

When Cobb finally put himself in the line-up on April 27, he went on a rampage that matched any of his career. On May 1, in an 8–7 loss at Cleveland, he banged out 4 hits, including a double. The next day, as his team lost by the same score, Cobb collected 3 more hits and scored twice. Two days later in St. Louis, Cobb ripped 2 hits in a one-run loss to the Browns. But with the Tigers resting 8½ games out of first already, Cobb was angry. The following day in the visitor's clubhouse, Cobb held court with several sportswriters, including his friend H. G. Salsinger from Detroit, and Sid Keener of the *St. Louis Star*. After one writer asked him for his reaction to Babe Ruth's continued absence from the Yankee line-up due to an illness, Cobb bristled. "All I hear about is Ruth and the home run ball. Everybody seems to forget the art of baseball—the science of it. I'll show you something today. I'm going for home runs for the first time in my career."[16]

That afternoon, with Cobb's words ringing in their ears, the sportswriters watched in awe as Cobb kept his promise. In the first inning, Cobb connected against Browns pitcher Bullet Joe Bush, launching a home run into the right-field bleachers. In the second, Cobb duplicated the blast, hitting the ball in nearly the same location for a second homer. In the fourth inning, Cobb lined a single over the second baseman's head for his third base hit. In the sixth inning, Cobb again slugged for power, sending a pitch to deep right center field that bounced near the wall. He cruised into second base with a double. Then, in the eighth inning, Cobb stunned the St. Louis crowd when he smacked a pitch from Elam Van Gilder over the right-field stands and into the street. It was his third homer of the contest. When Cobb came to bat for the final time in the ninth inning, the crowd gave him a standing ovation. Ty responded by tipping his cap. He then showed off his craftiness by bouncing a grounder to the hole at second base, which he easily beat out for a single. The Tigers won 14–8, and Cobb had entered the record books again. His three home runs in one game was something that even Ruth hadn't accomplished. His 6 for 6 performance was a record. His 16 total bases set a major league record that stood for years. He had driven in 7 runs and scored 4, in one of baseball's most incredible one-man performances.

The next afternoon, with baseball still buzzing over his uncharacteristic power display, Cobb gave them more. In the first inning, Cobb sent a line drive sharply to center for his ninth consecutive base hit. In the fifth inning, Cobb flexed his muscles again, belting a deep home run to right field off Dave Danforth. Two innings later, Cobb did it again, victimizing reliever Chet Falk for another home run. It was Cobb's fifth home run in two games, breaking a record held jointly by three others, including Ruth. In his final time at bat, Cobb thrilled the crowd when he sent a fly ball to deep right that nearly left the yard again. He had to settle for three hits in six trips to the plate in Detroit's 11–4 rout. His prodigious outburst of 9 hits, including 5 homers—in two games, had driven his season average to the astronomical height of .526. The following day, in the finale of the three-game set against the Browns, Cobb was held to a 1-for-4 performance by Frank "Dixie" Davis, his lone hit a double in the first inning which missed leaving the field by less than a foot.

Cobb had made his point. If he set his mind to it, he could hit the home run. But it was not his preference, and he wouldn't tally another homer for almost an entire month. He quickly returned to his style of slashing the ball and spraying it to all fields. By the end of June, the 38-year-old Cobb was hitting .410 to lead the league. His right fielder, Harry Heilmann, was nipping at his heels, and with the two outfielders leading the way, the Tigers crept toward the first division as the season wore on. In late May, the team won eleven of thirteen games, topping 10 runs scored in six of the victories. In mid-June, Cobb's club won nine straight—the longest streak of his managerial tenure to that point. Included in that stretch was the game of June 17 at Yankee Stadium, where the Tigers thrashed New York 19–1. Cobb belted a homer in that game, and went 4 for 4 with another home run the next day. He seemed to be challenging Ruth at his own game.

But the Senators and Athletics were well in front of the Tigers and Yankees in the AL race. Connie Mack had finally rebuilt his team, stocking it with players who would help him to later win three consecutive pennants. Without Ruth for the first two months of the season, the Yankees were helpless, and eventually finished well out of the running in seventh place.

Spurred by his fine hitting, Cobb's aggressive nature was rekindled in 1925. On July 8, in Detroit, Cobb and Howard Ehmke renewed their mutual disdain. When the pitcher, now with the Red Sox, galloped to first base to cover the bag on a routine sacrifice, Cobb crashed into him with full force, spiking him on the leg. The former teammates exchanged angry words and had to be separated. Three days later, in a game against the Yankees at Navin Field, Cobb was ejected after arguing with home plate umpire Pants Rowland—the former AL manager and a foe of Cobb's—over a strike call. Cobb was so upset that he bumped Rowland and later threw dirt on the umpire. His outburst earned him a five-day suspension from the league office.

For the month of July, Cobb batted just .300, as his season batting average slipped several points behind Heilmann, and that of his other outfielder, Absalom "Red" Wingo, who was also hitting among the league leaders. Unhappy with his production, Cobb benched himself and placed Heinie Manush in center field. In late August and early September, Detroit enjoyed a ten-game winning streak, but Cobb started in just six of those games. He used himself sparingly in the final month of the season, appearing in nineteen games after September 1, and making just 48 trips to the plate. His decision to curtail his own playing time was remarkable considering that he was still in the batting race. After Heilmann had slumped in early September, Cobb crept to within four points of the new batting leader, Tris Speaker. But Heilmann went on a hitting binge in the final week of the season to fly past both Cobb and Speaker and win his third batting title.

The season came to a close with a double-header in St. Louis on October 4. Cobb gathered 6 hits and even pitched a little in relief as the Tigers swept both games. The victories kept Detroit in fourth place, with a final record of 81–73. They had won five fewer games than the previous season. Once again the offense was exemplary; the team batted .302, the fourth time in Cobb's five years as manager that the club had reached the .300 level. Heilmann's late-season charge had lifted his average to .393. Red Wingo had hit .370, Lu Blue hit .306, and Bob Fothergill (.353) and Heinie Manush (.302) once again proved to be a solid platoon combination. The Tigers had scored a league-best 903 runs in 1925, but their team ERA ranked sixth in the American League. Hooks Dauss was the only Bengals hurler who enjoyed a quality season.

Cobb had played his fewest games since taking over as manager, despite a lofty .378 batting average. His power outburst at St. Louis in May had led him to a career-high 12 homers. He also drove in 102 runs and scored 97 times in just 121 games. He was still a very effective offensive player, despite his diminishing defensive abilities. Even though he was the oldest position player in the league, Cobb ranked second in the AL in on-base percentage and third in slugging.

After attending the 1925 World Series, which was won by the Pittsburgh Pirates in seven games, Cobb signed a one-year contract to manage the Tigers in 1926. Cobb and Navin's relationship had deteriorated considerably, but both men needed each other. Cobb still desired the attention he received at the helm of the Tigers, and Navin coveted the fans who flocked to the park to cheer the Georgia Peach.

In late October, Cobb hunted in Canada once more, and then headed home to Georgia. Later that winter, Cobb spent time hunting with Robert Woodruff, the president of Coca-Cola. Woodruff, who had succeeded his father as the head of the growing soft drink company, became one of Cobb's closest confidants. The two men were nearly the exact same age, and had both been born and raised in rural Georgia. Like Cobb, Woodruff had been "an indifferent student," preferring the excitement of the outdoors to schoolwork. Similar to Cobb, Woodruff had clashed with his father at an early age, and decided to go off on his own rather than follow his father's blueprint for him. But in 1923, Woodruff took over his father's company, and within a few years he had helped set it on a path toward even greater profit. This was of great interest to Cobb, who held tens of thousands of shares in the company. Several times during and after his playing career, Cobb joined Woodruff for hunting trips on his massive plantation in southwest Georgia.[17]

Early in March of 1926, Cobb had surgery to remove growths that had spread over each of his eyes. The ailment, known as "proud flesh," had hampered him the previous season, which made his .378 batting average even more amazing. The procedure delayed Cobb's arrival at spring training, which was once again held in Augusta. When Cobb joined his team, he began working quite a bit with Charlie Gehringer, who he felt was ready to take over at second base. When the veterans on the team tried to shut Gehringer out of the batting sessions—a common practice imposed on rookies—Cobb intervened. "Cobb was calling me in. I figured he wanted me to get out of the way. When I came in, he said,

'Get in there and hit again.' By this time the regulars were taking batting practice, and they didn't like the idea of me getting in with them. They didn't like that one bit. But it was Cobb's orders. I stepped in and started hitting again. This time Cobb wouldn't take his eyes off me; I could feel him staring at me."[18]

But the extra-time Cobb spent with Gehringer eventually backfired on the young second baseman. Gehringer learned that Cobb was very sensitive, even as a manager. One bad word or misunderstanding landed a player in Cobb's doghouse. Sometime in the spring of 1926, Cobb became miffed with Gehringer, and the two of them scarcely exchanged a word the rest of the season. Cobb was so peeved that he didn't play Gehringer regularly until second baseman Frank O'Rourke came down with the measles in June. "He was awfully touchy," Gehringer recalled, "I don't think anybody really got along with him. Of course, he'd never pick on Heilmann, say; Heilmann was too big a star. Cobb would pick on guys he knew couldn't battle back with him."[19]

One of the other young players in the Tigers camp that spring was left-handed pitcher Carl Hubbell, whose contract had been purchased from the Oklahoma City team. Cobb liked Hubbell's form, but he felt Hubbell needed more seasoning before being shoved into the big-league fire. A few years later, after Cobb had left Detroit, the Tigers ignored his glowing reports and released Hubbell, who went on to a Hall of Fame career with the New York Giants.

The veterans in camp in 1926 were the same players Cobb had failed to win with in previous years. Cobb was certain his offense would be potent, but without pitching help it wouldn't mean a thing. Detroit would once again rely on Whitehill, Dauss, and the same cast of characters on the mound. As the team traveled north to begin the regular season, Cobb had determined that he would play very little in 1926. His outfield was deep, boasting Heilmann, Manush, Fothergill, and Wingo, and he felt his talents were best suited for pinch hitting and full-time managing from the bench.

On April 13 in Detroit, with Cobb's wife and five children in the stands, the Tigers opened the season with a heartbreaking 2–1 loss to the Indians. Whitehill pitched well enough to win, but the Bengals bats were silenced by Cleveland hurler George Uhle. Cobb pinch hit late in the contest, hitting into a double play. On April 27, after the team had lost seven of their first eleven games, Cobb finally penned his own name into the starting line-up. The 39-year-old had a banner day, going 3 for 4 with a double and a triple, 4 RBIs, and 2 runs scored. He also made a dazzling running catch in center field to preserve an 8–7 triumph.

In May, the Tigers played much better, going 17–12 for the month as Cobb's bat heated up. That month, Cobb hit in twenty-one straight games to hoist his season average to .398. On May 9 in Yankee Stadium, he socked 2 home runs among his 4 hits. Over one seven-game stretch, he hit .469 with 15 base hits. By that time, Gehringer was out of Cobb's doghouse and in the starting line-up. In his first full season, the future Hall-of-Famer hit .277 with a team-high 17 triples, while playing splendidly in the field.

On June 11, after a rough stretch, Detroit found themselves in sixth place, 14 games behind Ruth's Yankees; Cobb had played in 45 of his club's 55 games. But from that point on he appeared in just 34 of the final 99 games, as he turned center field over to Manush, who was enjoying a breakout season. On July 6, against catcher Luke Sewell of the Indians, Cobb stole home for the last time in a Tigers uniform. On August 20, in the first game of a double-header, Cobb went 3 for 4 in what would be his final start of the season. During the balance of the campaign, Cobb sent himself in as a pinch hitter or defensive replacement.

As the season dragged on, having more time from the bench to devote his attention to nonplaying matters, Cobb feuded with umpires, opposing players, his own players, and the fans. The love-hate relationship with the public that Cobb enjoyed as Tigers manager was leaning heavily toward hate in the latter stages of 1926. "Ty Cobb has lost his popularity in this city," one sportswriter noted, "and there are hundreds, yes, even thousands of fans who attend the games at Navin Field in hopes of having a chance to boo and jeer their former idol."[20] Cobb seemed to care little, as he took out his frustrations on his team. "He was tough to play for and very demanding," Gehringer recalled. "He was so great himself that he couldn't understand why if he told players how to do certain things, they couldn't do it as well as he did. But if you had the talent, then he could really help you. I think he made a fine hitter of Manush, who pretty much followed Cobb's advice, and of course, had the talent to take advantage of it."[21] Manush withstood Cobb's tirades in 1926 to win his first batting title. On the last day of the season, in a meaningless double-header against the Red Sox, Manush collected 6 hits to nip Ruth for the crown, delighting Cobb.

The Tigers finished in sixth place with a 79–75 record, 12 games behind the Yankees. Cobb had played in just 79 games, batting .339 with 4 home runs and 48 runs scored. In spite of his little playing time, he was valuable in the clutch, driving in 62 runs, the fourth highest total on the team behind his trio of regular outfielders. Manush had hit .378, Heilmann .367, Fothergill .367, and catcher Johnny Bassler, before an injury shelved him, also topped .300. But the pitching and defense had not been good enough to make Detroit a contender.

Cobb had managed six seasons and never reached higher than second place. Attendance in Detroit had slipped, and rumors were flying that Navin would fire Cobb or that Ty would retire. As he packed his belongings for the trip back to Georgia, Cobb did little to squash the rumors. He was fed up with Navin, whom he blamed for not having purchased any top-notch pitchers. Cobb was also tired of the strain that managing placed on him. When he left for Augusta, Ty hinted that he had played his final baseball game.

On November 4, the news of Cobb's resignation hit the newspapers. Cobb had delivered his resignation letter to Navin in Detroit and then quietly returned to Georgia. His days in baseball seemed to have come to an end. During the off-season, Cobb reminisced about his playing career. "Give me the legs of the young fellow I was fifteen years ago and I might make some records, but that's impossible now."[22]

Navin replaced Cobb with George Moriarty, a former ball player and American League umpire, as well as a teammate of Cobb's from 1909 to 1915. Moriarty had written a book titled *Don't Die on Third*, that outlined his baseball philosophy, which hinged largely on the stolen base. In 1927, Moriarty's Tigers swiped 141 bases, the highest total by a Detroit club since 1917, and roughly double the number the team had stolen per year under Cobb. But the pilfering did little to save Moriarty's job; he was fired two years later with a sub-.500 record in two seasons at the helm.

Cobb's six years as manager had been exciting, if unsuccessful for the team. The club had consistently fielded the best hitters in the league. Cobb's players won four batting championships in his six seasons, while Ty hit over .300 himself every year as a player-manager. His final record as a manager was 479 wins against 444 losses, for a .519 winning percentage. His best squad, the 1923 team, had finished sixteen games out of first place. He had been a difficult man to play for and a difficult man for Navin to deal with, but he had drawn large crowds for most of his years at the helm. Still, his accomplishments as a manager had been less than remarkable. Where he was a fantastic evaluator of hitting talent and was perhaps the greatest batting coach in the game, he was a poor handler of pitchers. His personal differences with some of his players had sabotaged his team's success, and kept him from achieving his goal of a pennant.

On December 18, 1926, Cobb celebrated his fortieth birthday. For the first time in twenty-three years, he didn't have a baseball team to report to the following spring. It seemed that the Georgia Peach was through.

NOTES

1. Marc Okkonen, *The Ty Cobb Scrapbook: An Illustrated Chronology of Significant Dates In the 24-Year Career of the Fabled Georgia Peach; Over 800 Games From 1905 to 1928* (New York: Sterling Publishing Co., 2001), 149.

2. *Baseball Magazine*, December 1926, 399–400.

3. Cobb, with Stump, *My Life in Baseball*, 187.

4. *New York Times*, May 14, 1922, 27.

5. *St. Louis Post-Dispatch*, June 25, 1921, 17.

6. Fred Lieb, *Baseball As I Have Known It* (New York: Coward, McCann and Geoghegan, 1977), 68.

7. *New York Monitor*, October 11, 1922, 26.

8. Quote by E. A. Batchelor, unknown source, Ty Cobb file, National Baseball Hall of Fame Library.

9. Quote by E. A. Batchelor, unknown source, Ty Cobb file, National Baseball Hall of Fame Library.

10. Honig, *Baseball When the Grass Was Real*, 43–44.

11. Ted Lyons file, National Baseball Hall of Fame Library.

12. Cobb, with Stump, *My Life in Baseball*, 105.

13. Okkonen, *The Ty Cobb Scrapbook*, 161.

14. Alexander, *Ty Cobb*, 173.

15. *Sporting News*, July 5, 1950, 16.

16. *Sporting News*, December 27, 1961, 11–12.

17. Robert W. Woodruff Foundation, www.woodruff.org/biography.html.

18. Honig, *Baseball When the Grass Was Real*, 44.

19. Ibid., 44–45.

20. *Cleveland Plain Dealer*, June 27, 1926, 1B.

21. Charlie Gehringer file, National Baseball Hall of Fame Library.

22. *Baseball Magazine*, January 1927, 340.

Cobb, wearing a suit, looks over one of his golfing irons. *National Baseball Hall of Fame Library, Cooperstown, N.Y.*

7

SCANDAL AND REDEMPTION

Just three days after Ty Cobb's fortieth birthday, on December 21, 1926, the news of his retirement took a back seat to shocking details coming out of Chicago. Cobb and Tris Speaker had been implicated in a gambling scandal that threatened to ruin their reputation. The commissioner's office released documents that alleged that Cobb and Speaker had been part of a scheme to throw one of the final games of the 1919 season. The fix was designed to ensure that Detroit would finish in third place and receive postseason money. The allegations came from Dutch Leonard, the left-handed pitcher who had been a teammate of Ty's in 1919, and later pitched for Cobb in 1921 and 1924–1925. Leonard had grown to hate Cobb, and had always distrusted Ty, dating back to his days as a member of the Boston Red Sox pitching staff in the 1910s. Leonard had been one of the Boston hurlers who had treated Cobb like a pin cushion, aiming fastballs at Ty's body.

The commissioner had a pair of letters from Leonard that the pitcher claimed were proof that he, Cobb, Speaker, and Boston pitcher Joe Wood, had conspired to throw the game of September 25, 1919. Furthermore, Leonard said that the four players had each planned to bet on the Tigers to win the game. But the man chosen to place the bets, a Navin Field employee, was unable to get most of the money down on Detroit in time. Consequently, none of the players made much on what they had allegedly put at stake: $2,000 by Cobb, $1,500 by Leonard, and $1,000 each for Speaker and Wood. The Tigers ended up winning the contest 9–5, but newspaper accounts of the game failed to reveal there had been any suspicious play. According to Leonard, the four men each won approximately $500, which was split between the man who had placed the bets, Wood, Speaker, and Leonard. Cobb never got a dime.

The story was damaging to the men involved and potentially disastrous for the game of baseball. Former federal judge Kenesaw Mountain Landis, a stodgy disciplinarian, had helped rid baseball of the gambling element since his election as commissioner in 1920. The "Black Sox Scandal," which had ended the career of eight Chicago players, including Joe Jackson, had rocked baseball in 1920. A scandal involving Cobb and Speaker—two of baseball's greatest legends—would be devastating.

It didn't take long for Cobb to respond to the "sickening affair," as he called it.[1] Within a few days, Cobb had hired his lawyers to sue the commissioner of baseball, as well as AL President Ban Johnson. "I hope God will vent his curse upon me if I ever did one dishonest thing in baseball," Cobb said. "How can any sane man believe Leonard for even a second? Look at the facts."[2] The facts supported Cobb's denial of any wrongdoing. A disgruntled Leonard had contacted Landis in May of 1926, hoping to damage Cobb and Speaker, both of whom he felt had blackballed him from the major leagues. Leonard claimed Cobb had overused him and hurt his arm, and that Speaker had refused to sign him to pitch for Cleveland. There was evidence that as far back as 1921, Leonard was scheming to "get back" at Cobb. In addition, the facts surrounding the game itself were very peculiar. If the Indians had actually been trying to lose to the Tigers, why did Speaker have what Cobb called "a field day" at the plate, with three hits? How could four players, two of whom (Leonard and Wood) were not even playing, have thrown the game?

Later, after Cobb's lawyers and the newspapers began to press the issue, it came to light that Johnson had paid Leonard to keep quiet about the entire affair, so it could be handled behind closed doors. The revelation did more to damage Johnson and Landis than it did Cobb or Speaker, who by this time were receiving overwhelming support throughout the country. In Washington D.C., Georgia Senator William H. Harris vowed to investigate the allegations and exonerate Cobb. Former teammates and opposing players rallied to defend Cobb and Speaker, as did Billy Evans, the umpire whom Cobb had fought so savagely under the stands in 1921. Cobb found unusual allies in Babe Ruth and John McGraw, two foes against whom he battled for many years. Back in his home state, thousands of supporters came to Cobb's defense. In a rare public appearance, his wife spoke out on his behalf as well. "I know him better than anyone else," Charlotte Cobb said. "He has lived clean and played the game clean."[3]

In January of 1927, new rumors of gambling, fixes, and thrown games were surfacing every day. It seemed as if every unsavory character who had ever played the game was coming out of the woodwork to tell their story of fixed games and payoffs. All of the allegations dated back several years, before Landis had been appointed commissioner. As the negative publicity piled higher, Landis grew anxious to resolve the Cobb-Speaker affair.

After he held hearings to dig deeper into some of the new allegations, Landis exonerated Cobb and Speaker in a written statement on January 27. "These players have not been, nor are they now, found guilty of fixing a ball game. By no decent system of justice could such a finding be made."[4] Landis also declared that he had determined that Johnson had pressured the Tigers and Indians to get rid of Cobb and Speaker, respectively. He restored both of the players to their active status, effective immediately. Landis made his swift and sweeping action to restore confidence in the game, to ensure that two of the game's greatest players were not wrongfully tainted, and to assert his power over Johnson. Landis and Johnson had struggled over power before, and the defeat for Johnson in the Cobb-Speaker affair proved fatal. In October of 1927, Johnson was removed as president of the American League.

The Tigers gave Cobb free-agent status almost immediately, with Cleveland doing the same for Speaker. Neither player would return to their former teams, but at least their reputations had been saved. Relieved that he had been vindicated, Cobb made no indication that he would ever play again: "I have played in more ball games than any other major leaguer who ever lived. Doesn't that entitle me to a rest?"[5] But soon several teams were clamoring to get Cobb's name on a contract. The Brooklyn Dodgers wanted his star appeal in the National League. McGraw of the Giants expressed interest as well. The Browns and Senators offered tens of thousands of dollars for Cobb to be a player-coach, and Jack Dunn, the maverick owner of the Baltimore Orioles in the International League, tried to entice Cobb to play on his club.

At the end of January, when Speaker signed a one-year deal with the Senators, fans waited anxiously to see where Cobb would end up. A few days later, A's owner Connie Mack visited Ty and Charlotte Cobb in Augusta. Mack had several good young ballplayers on his team and he was poised to get back in the thick of things in the AL, after several years of last-place finishes. The wise old man of the game, who had battled with the Tigers and a young Cobb nearly twenty years earlier in what Ty called his "greatest game," convinced Cobb that he had at least one more good season in his body. Cobb was attracted by the prospect of proving himself after the gambling accusations. He also liked the notion of playing on a winning ballclub. In 1926, Mack's A's had won just four more games than Cobb's Tigers, but they were loaded with talent, and best of all they had pitching, something a Cobb team hadn't enjoyed in several years.

Mack had to outbid Brooklyn and a few other National League clubs for Cobb's services, but he finally got the veteran's name on a contract in early February. Ty would earn $40,000 in 1927 for Philadelphia, and another $30,000 in the form of a signing bonus and incentives should the team's gate reach a certain plateau. It was one of a number of headline-grabbing deals Mack orchestrated that off-season. Veteran Eddie Collins, who had began his career with Mack, also signed a one-year deal to return to Philadelphia. In addition, Mack landed outfielder Zack Wheat, the 38-year old former batting champion, who had spent his entire career with the Dodgers. "Mack signed Zack Wheat, Eddie Collins, and Ty Cobb—a six-legged, one-hundred-and-sixteen-year-old veteran with sixty-one years of experience."[6] The three free agents proved worthy; combined, the trio of veterans would hit .344 for Mack in 1927.

In early March, Cobb arrived for spring training in Fort Myers, Florida, joining his new Athletics' teammates. He gave every indication that it would be his last season in uniform. The team was a mixture of young stars and aging veterans. The starting catcher was 24-year-old Mickey Cochrane, a fiery player with a good bat and a strong throwing arm. Al Simmons, the 25-year-old center fielder, owned a .347 batting average in three seasons in the big leagues. The pitching staff was led by Robert Moses "Lefty" Grove, a 27-year-old southpaw who had won nearly 100 games for Dunn in the International League before Mack snatched him for a hefty price. Forty-year-old Cobb and 38-year-old Wheat figured to play in the outfield with Simmons, while Collins, who was also 40 years old, was set to share the second base chores with "Camera Eye" Max Bishop.

Mack used Cobb in right field during the spring, with Simmons in center and either Wheat or "Good Time Bill" Lamar in left. In April, Cobb and his family traveled north a few days before the rest of the team to find a home in Philadelphia. They found a nice home in the northwest suburbs of the city, just a short distance from Shibe Park, the A's home field since 1909.

On April 12, the A's began the 1927 season in New York against the Yankees. Cobb wore the gray flannels of the Philadelphia Athletics—trimmed in dark blue, with a white elephant on the left breast. The elephant had been a franchise symbol since the early 1900s, when John McGraw sneered at the upstart American League as a bunch of "white elephants."[7] Batting third and playing right field in front of a huge opening day crowd in Yankee Stadium, Cobb collected a single and a walk as the A's lost 8–3. It was the first of twenty-three meetings between the two clubs that season. Between them, the A's and Yankees had thirteen future Hall-of-Famers in uniform, and two more on the sidelines in managers Mack and Miller Huggins.

Without the headaches and responsibilities that came with managing to bother him, Cobb was rejuvenated. He hit safely in his first seven games, and on April 21 he started a 21-game hitting streak in which he batted .449 with 9 doubles, 3 triples, 1 homer, 18 runs, and 19 RBIs. The spurt vaulted him to the top of the AL batting charts. In an April game against Washington, Cobb learned the depth of Mr. Mack's baseball knowledge. With Mack waving Cobb to play deeper in center field against Goose Goslin, Cobb finally acquiesced, and to his surprise, Goslin's ensuing drive landed harmlessly in his glove. Upon his arrival in the Athletics' dugout, Cobb grinned and said, "That's the first time anyone's told me where to stand. Mr. Mack, you had it exactly right."[8]

On May 10, Cobb returned to Detroit for the first time in an enemy uniform. The city of Detroit rolled out the red carpet, with the mayor and other dignitaries greeting Cobb as he entered the city. More than 27,000 fans turned out at Navin Field for "Ty Cobb Day," which was preceded by a small parade. Prior to the game, Cobb received several gifts from his admirers in Detroit, including a new automobile and a silver serving set. In the first inning, with a runner on first, Cobb lofted an Earl Whitehill pitch into right field for a double, and later scored on a base hit as Detroit fans cheered for their longtime hero. In the four-game series against his former team, Cobb went 5 for 13 with 4 doubles, as Philadelphia won three times.

In spite of Cobb's outstanding hitting in May, the A's were a meager 13–15 during the month, which left them six games back of the Yankees. In a five-game series that started on May 30, the A's lost four times to the Yankees, once by a score of 18–5. In mid-June, the risks of employing older players haunted Mack, with Cobb and Collins both suffering injuries. Cobb strained his hip while running out a routine ground ball to short, and Collins pulled a hamstring. After missing a double-header, Cobb returned on June 22, but Mack only used him as pinch hitter for a week. While he was out, the A's slumped and fell to fifth place, fourteen games behind the Yankees, who were having an historic season. Then on July 10, Cobb had four hits in a 14–11 slugfest over the Browns, and added three more hits the next day, including a home run. A few weeks later, Mack moved Cobb to center field and the cleanup slot in his line-up after Simmons suffered an injury that kept him out for six weeks.

But for a 40-year-old man, the strain of playing center field got to be too much at times. In one stretch that included a series against the Tigers, Cobb went 0 for 20. Cobb's legs were tired from the years of abuse, and his back and arms became increasingly sore as the season unfolded. He started to spend more time in bed between games, conserving his energy.

But when he chose to unleash his energy, Cobb was still a thrilling ballplayer. In one game, he singled, stole second, and scampered all the way home when the catcher threw wildly to center. In another contest, in August, Cobb singled and scored all the way from first when the right fielder bobbled a routine single. As the fielder struggled to get the ball in his glove, he was surprised to see Cobb barreling around third. The resulting throw was well up the line toward third base and Cobb tiptoed across the plate.

On July 18 in Detroit, Cobb collected his 4,000th career hit, a double off Sam Gibson. Like his 3,000th hit, the milestone was barely noted in the news at the time. With 4,000 hits to his credit, the Georgia Peach was more than 600 hits ahead of Speaker, who was second on the all-time list. For nearly sixty years, Cobb would be the only man to reach the 4,000 hit plateau, until Pete Rose joined him in 1984.

In August and September, Cobb hit with consistency, batting safely in 25 of 28 games in one stretch. Philadelphia played well in August—winning 21 of 28 games to move into second place. But the Yankees were 17 games ahead, with Babe Ruth and Lou Gehrig leading the way with their record-setting home run exploits. In September, the A's continued their winning ways, while Cobb pounded out 26 hits in 18 games for the month. But that was the extent of Cobb's contribution, as he left the team on September 21 to return to Georgia. With the Yankees having secured the pennant, Mack had agreed to let the veteran Cobb get an early start on the off-season. Cobb stole 6 bases and hit .586 (17 for 29) in his last week of action to lift his final season average to .357, a figure that would prove to be fifth in the league. He drove in 93 runs in 134 games, with 34 doubles, 7 triples, and 5 home runs. Despite his early exit, he led the team with 104 runs scored, and his 22 steals were good for third in the AL.

At 40 years old, Cobb had proven that he had plenty of good baseball left in his tired body. For his efforts, which helped the A's to 91 wins and a second-place finish, Cobb was rewarded. According to Connie Mack Jr., his father paid Cobb $70,000 for the 1927 season—$20,000 as a signing bonus, $40,000 in salary, and $10,000 as part of a clause which kicked in if the A's won the pennant. Even though the A's did not win the pennant in 1927, Mack was so pleased with Cobb's performance and his gate appeal that he paid the bonus to his aging star.[9]

After several weeks of traveling, Cobb and his wife returned to Augusta, where Ty fielded questions about his future. He wasn't sure if he wanted to play another season, and he also wasn't sure if any team wanted him at what would be an expensive price tag. In December he turned 41 years old, and with his prosperous business ventures and his hunting dogs, Cobb had more than enough to keep him busy.

But baseball always seemed to be on his mind. His old friend, Clark Griffith of the Washington Senators, tried to coax Cobb back for one more season, and Brooklyn and Chicago of the National League were also rumored to have their feelers out. In February, Tris Speaker, who had enjoyed a fine season in Washington the year before, signed a one-year contract with Mack to play for the A's. Mack told reporters that he still wanted Cobb back, if they could agree on terms. Mack signed Speaker for $35,000, half of what he had paid Cobb in 1927. If he could get Cobb to come back for the same amount, he'd have two veteran stars for the price it had cost him for one the year before.

Eventually, after Mack paid another visit to the Cobb's in Augusta, Ty relented and signed for nearly what Speaker had accepted. Mack had secured the services of the two greatest outfielders in baseball history. Cobb had decided to come back for a twenty-fourth major league season, more than any man had ever played. Though he hardly needed the money and he wasn't looking forward to the physical rigors of another season, Cobb was drawn by the possibility of playing on a World Series team. His three World Series appearances had happened in his youth, and he was thirsty for the opportunity to play in that spotlight once again, as a veteran ballplayer. In addition, Cobb loved the prospect of playing in the same outfield with Speaker.

In the spring of 1928, in Fort Myers, Mack played Simmons in left field, Speaker in center, and Cobb in right. The two veterans took their time getting their bodies in shape for one more season of baseball. Throughout the spring, wherever the team went, invariably Cobb, Speaker, Collins, and 44-year-old pitcher Jack Quinn, were grouped together for publicity shots. Mack's aging stars were the talk of baseball. If the quartet could translate into notches in the win column and fans in the seats, Mack would be happy.

In 1928, the A's had some good outfield talent that sat on the bench as Cobb and Speaker wrapped up their Hall-of-Fame careers. 22-year-old Roger "Doc" Cramer, who would go on to collect more than 2,700 hits in a 20-year career, failed to get into a single game for Mack that year, but Cobb made an impression on him. "A lot of people didn't like Cobb, but that never seemed to bother him. Anyway, he was very nice to me. I liked him."[10]

On April 11, the Athletics opened the season at home against the Yankees, whom they figured to battle for AL supremacy. Lefty Grove was battered for an 8–3 loss in the game, as Cobb went 1 for 3 with two walks off Herb Pennock. Mack used Cobb in the second spot in his order, with Speaker and Simmons batting behind him; Max Bishop was the leadoff man. On April 20, after four losses to open the season, Cobb and Speaker teamed to defeat New York in Yankee Stadium. With the game deadlocked, Cobb produced a thundering triple to deep center field to open the ninth inning, and came into score on Speaker's sacrifice fly. The run proved to be the winning margin in Philadelphia's 2–1 victory. The next day, Cobb had three hits in a 10–0 pasting of the Yankees, and two days later he started an eleven-game hitting streak that coincided with the team winning thirteen of fourteen. But despite their hot streak, Cobb and the

A's were still trailing the Yankees in the standings. With Ruth and Gehrig, the Yankees were rolling to a great start once again.

On May 16, Cobb hit a home run against Cleveland at Shibe Park in a 15–2 triumph. It would be the final home run of his career. As Mack's team made their way around the league, sportswriters noted the slowed play of both Cobb and Speaker. Even though the two outfielders were keeping their averages above the .300 mark, it was obvious to observers that their skills had eroded. In one game against the Red Sox, Cobb and Speaker converged on a ball hit to medium right field, only to have it drop between them for a double. It was a play that each of them could have made from center field in their prime. In May, Speaker was injured when he collided with Edmund "Bing" Miller, and missed several weeks of action. To compensate for the aging legs of his star outfielders, Mack shuttled Miller and George "Mule" Haas in and out of the lineup.

On the base paths, Cobb was taking fewer chances, but when he did he was more likely to be thrown out. For the season, the once fleet-footed threat was caught stealing 8 times in 13 tries. But Cobb still had a few tricks up his sleeves. On June 15 in Cleveland, he worked his way around to third base and then dashed in to steal home against the stunned Indian battery. It was his 35th career swipe of home, and his last. In a game against the Browns, Cobb looped a single to center field and took advantage of the lackadaisical play of outfielder Ken Williams, who lazily fielded the ball with his head down. Charging around the bag, Cobb hustled to second base, sliding safely in a flash of spikes.

In July, Cobb's bat cooled off and he suffered a number of nagging injuries, which left him incapable of playing on an everyday basis. From that point on he played primarily from the bench, getting into action as a pinch hitter when Mack waved a bony finger in his direction. Joining him on the bench were Speaker and Collins, who had been relegated to part-time duty earlier. The only "old man" who proved to be consistently valuable to Mack was pitcher Jack Quinn, who was among the league leaders in ERA all season.

At the end of July, spurred by the hitting of Simmons and the dominant pitching of Grove, Quinn, and Eddie Rommel, Mack's team was within five and one-half games of the Yankees. After a fine showing in August, Mack's team had won forty-four of sixty-one games to inch within two games of New York. With his younger players carrying the club to contention, Mack left Cobb and the others on the bench, going to them rarely. On September 3 against Washington, Cobb collected the final hit of his career, stroking a double off Irving "Bump" Hadley, a 23-year-old right-hander.

A five-game winning streak in early September lifted the Mackmen into first place, and it looked as if Cobb might get his chance to return to the Fall Classic. But in a crucial four-game match against the Yankees that followed, Philadelphia lost three in a row. Even though they salvaged the finale 4–3, the losses proved fatal. The Yankees kept winning and the A's couldn't gain any ground. In the critical series against the Yankees, Cobb made his final major league appearance, pinch hitting for Jimmie Dykes. Batting against right-hander Hank Johnson in the top of the ninth, Cobb popped a lazy fly ball to short left field that was gathered in by shortstop Mark Koenig. His final stats for the 1928 season: 95 games played, 114 hits, 27 doubles, 4 triples, 1 homer, 40 RBIs, 5 steals, and a .323 batting average. At the age of 41, Cobb had hit over .300 for the 23rd consecutive season.

When the A's went into Detroit for their final three-games against the Tigers on September 20, Cobb sat on the bench at Navin Field, coming out only to tip his cap to the fans. Two days earlier, he had announced that he would retire for good following the season. "I'm just baseball tired and want to quit," he said.[11]

On September 27, with the Athletics eliminated from the pennant race, Cobb wore his uniform one last time before heading home to Georgia. There was no tearful farewell, no special send-off. Ty Cobb, the greatest player in baseball history, and the holder of dozens of records, had ended his amazing career. He was philosophical about his twenty-four years on the diamond: "I shall depart with one regret, and that is that I have done no real good for humanity. I suppose everybody will have forgotten me within a few years time."[12]

NOTES

1. Cobb, with Stump, *My Life in Baseball*, 242.
2. Ibid., 243.
3. Alexander, *Ty Cobb*, 189.
4. Ibid., 194.
5. *Baseball Magazine*, January 1927, 339.
6. Jim Kaplan, *Lefty Grove: American Original* (Cleveland: Society for American Baseball Research, 2000), 105.
7. McGraw had briefly been a manager in the American League in 1901–1902, but a feud with owners of the Baltimore franchise and Ban Johnson, the patriarch of the league, led McGraw to jump to the National League. His bitterness toward Johnson and the AL led to the decision by the Giants to forego the 1904 World Series.
8. Kaplan, *Lefty Grove*, 105.
9. Connie Mack file, National Baseball Hall of Fame Library.
10. Honig, *Baseball When the Grass Was Real*, 192.
11. *Philadelphia Inquirer*, September 18, 1928, 24.
12. *Sporting News*, July 5, 1950, 16.

LEGEND AND LOATHING

When Ty Cobb retired, he left baseball a different game than when he had entered it as a fresh-faced, 18-year-old rookie from rural Georgia. His revolutionary use of cunning and speed had transformed the game. He worked harder than any player ever had to squeeze every ounce of talent from his body. He put his legs through the ordeal of twenty-four major league seasons, running and sliding until his ankles and thighs had scars on top of scars. He sharpened his mind until it became a powerful instrument that he relied upon at the plate, on the basepaths, in the outfield, and in the dugout. He branded his strong personality on the game and lifted the sport to heights it had never seen. "He did more for baseball," Ban Johnson said, "than any single individual that ever lived. The game owes him more than it will ever realize."[1]

But the game Cobb left in 1928 was much different than it had been in the glory days of the Georgia Peach. The home run had become paramount, pushing the intricate game of finesse and strategy to the side. Because it had been his exceptional finesse and strategic mastery that had elevated Cobb to the top of the baseball world, the rapidly changing emphasis on power-hitting made Cobb bitter toward the game in retirement. Throughout the years after his playing career ended, Cobb would chastise the "muscle guys who had overtaken the game.[2]

Conversely, on some occasions, Ty would emerge to congratulate the use of what he considered "inside baseball"—the hit-and-run, sacrifice bunt, stolen base, and defense. In 1959, just a few years before his death, Cobb wrote a letter on that subject to Al Lopez, the manager of the Chicago White Sox. Lopez had guided his team to the American League pennant, halting a four-year run by the Yankees. "You have done a wonderful job, you and your team," Cobb wrote. "I admire how you did it. You play a type of game I know so well."[3]

At times during Cobb's retirement, Cobb blasted the modern ballplayer. "The great trouble with baseball today is that most of the players are in the game for the money and that's it, not for the love of it, the excitement of it, the thrill of it." Cobb seemed to have forgotten his own frequent holdouts.[4]

In the immediate years following his retirement, from baseball, Cobb traveled, hunted, trained his dogs, and spent time with his five children. The *Sporting News* wrote, "Cobb's future is not known. He does not have to worry. He hailed a bat into Detroit in the Fall of 1905 that made more than a million dollars for him. He is the richest player baseball has ever known. Cobb was a shrewd investor and his earnings multiplied as a result of his wisdom in selecting the right kind of stocks. He got in both Coca Cola and General Motors on the ground floor."[5] He and Charlotte spent several months traveling through Europe and across the Americas. But the Cobb marriage was not a healthy one. In 1931, Charlotte Cobb filed for divorce, which came as a shock to Ty. Though it's not certain how strong a union his parents had enjoyed, Cobb was a believer in the sanctity of marriage. He had provided well for Charlotte and their five children, and even though his occupation had required that he travel several months out of the year, he had tried to be a good father and husband. But he was a difficult man to live with. Like his father, Cobb was a demanding figure who was quick to criticize. He was a nineteenth-century man who believed in traditional roles for husbands and wives, an attitude that increasingly rankled Charlotte Cobb as the years wore on. Charlotte was the product of a powerful family and had a strong will of her own.

But Cobb proved persuasive, and he succeeded in convincing Charlotte to stay with him. In 1932, Ty and Charlotte moved to Atherton, California, just outside of San Francisco, with their three youngest children, Herschel, Beverly, and Jimmy. The family still maintained their home in Augusta, but Cobb wished to live in a warmer climate that allowed him to partake in his second greatest athletic passion—golf. Cobb was never a great golfer, but he was skilled at hitting the ball a long distance with his short left-handed swing. When in California, he played nearly every day and gradually lowered his score. On the links he could be as nasty as he'd been on the basepaths. On one occasion while golfing at the exclusive Augusta National Golf Course in the 1950s, Cobb grew frustrated with a slow foursome in front of him and angrily launched his golf ball over their heads, shouting expletives as he went, the startled foursome included President Dwight D. Eisenhower. In the 1940s, Cobb and Babe Ruth renewed their rivalry when they toured the country playing a series of golf matches to support the war effort. Golf and polo were Cobb's favorite athletic pursuits in retirement. On the polo field, Cobb was a fierce player, relying on his aggressive and cunning nature, as well as his mastery of horses.

In the mid-1930s, civic leaders in Cooperstown, New York, hatched the idea of constructing a museum and hall of fame dedicated to baseball, in hopes of creating a tourist attraction. Armed with the myth that baseball had been invented in Cooperstown, and with the blessings of Commisioner Landis and Ford C. Frick, the president of the National League, the plan moved forward. In 1936, the Baseball Writers' Association of America held the first election for the Hall of Fame. When the 226 ballots were counted, Cobb had received votes on 222 of them, the highest total attained by any candidate. Babe Ruth and Honus Wagner each received 215 votes, Christy Mathewson tallied 205, and Walter Johnson was credited with 189. Those five, having achieved the requisite 75 percent support, would be the first men inducted into the National Baseball Hall of Fame and Museum. It was a proud moment for Cobb, who was delighted that he had received more support than any other player.

Less than eight months after receiving the news that he had been elected to the Hall of Fame, Cobb's mother Amanda died at the age of 65. Over the years, Cobb and his mother (as well as his sister Florence) had spent increasingly less time together. Cobb traveled back to Georgia for the burial, supervising the details of his mother's burial in the Royston cemetery, not far from William Herschel Cobb. Amanda Cobb had taken the secret of W. H. Cobb's death to the grave with her. If it had not been an accidental death, as Cobb maintained throughout his life, his mother kept it to herself.

On June 12, 1939, the Hall of Fame was officially dedicated in Cooperstown. By that time more players and managers had been selected in the annual elections, including Tris Speaker and Connie Mack. At the ceremonies that day, all of the living inductees in attendance posed for an historic photo, but Cobb missed the moment. He arrived later in the day, having missed much of the ceremony. He claimed later that he had delayed his arrival so he wouldn't have to be on the same stage as Landis, whom he still despised for the way he handled the 1926–1927 gambling fiasco. Cobb's youngest son, Jimmy, who traveled to Cooperstown with his father, insisted that they had been late because of unforeseen travel delays. Whatever the reason, it seems fitting that Cobb, who had been a loner and had often been cast as a villain during his playing days, was not in the historic photo.

Of Cobb's five children, Jimmy enjoyed the strongest relationship with his father. When his youngest son served in World War II, Cobb was extremely proud. Jimmy Cobb remembered that period of his life later on: "The memory that stands out for me was when the war ended and I came back from overseas to San Francisco, and my dad was waiting for me when my ship came in. He was waiting for me with three doughnuts and an ice-cold pitcher of milk. I hated [the] powdered milk that they gave us in the military and he knew it. I'm an emotional guy and I was really choked up when I saw him."[6] Later, after his father's death, Jimmy Cobb became the most vocal supporter of his father, defending Ty Cobb's legacy against critics.

In 1947, after several years of strained marriage, Charlotte finally divorced Ty Cobb. They had been married for nearly forty years and raised five children. During their marriage, Ty had accumulated a massive fortune through his shrewd investments and business ventures. Charlotte sued for half of Ty's money and a handsome monthly alimony payment. Eventually, the two avoided a drawn out legal battle and settled in court, filing a quick divorce in Reno, Nevada, where Ty owned a vacation home.

For the most part, Cobb's children were never close to their father. Ty Jr., the oldest, had the most difficult relationship with Ty. After a series of disappointments in college and on the athletic field, Ty Jr. became estranged from his father. The two rarely spoke with each other until 1951, when Ty Jr.—by then a successful doctor—was diagnosed with brain cancer. In the last few months of his life, Ty Jr. reconciled with his famous father. Their relationship had been eerily similar to that of Ty with his own father.

Herschel Cobb, Ty's next oldest son, had a more meaningful relationship with his father, though still distant. Herschel became a successful businessman, running a Coca-Cola bottling plant that Ty had set up for him. Tragically, in 1951, just a year before Ty Jr. died, Herschel died of a massive heart attack at the early age of 34. The loss of two of his sons within a short period was a stress on Cobb, and the knowledge that he had been a part-time and distant father was also difficult.

Both of Cobb's daughters, Shirley and Beverly, married and started families of their own. They had fond memories of their father when they were children, but found it difficult to relate to him as the years wore on. Following his death, they represented their father by attending Hall of Fame ceremonies in Cooperstown.

Following the early death of his oldest sons and the end of his marriage, Cobb withdrew from his family for much of the last decade of his life. He rarely saw his brother Paul or sister Florence, who both lived in Florida. Cobb became protective of his accomplishments in baseball, criticizing those who attacked his controversy-laden career. He showed no signs that he regretted the fiery temper he flashed on the diamond. "A tough, aggressive spirit never hurt anyone. That is, anyone able to rise above the inevitable slurs that such a spirit arouses. Embattled men often forfeit some happiness. But the knowledge that they never backed down from any challenge will warm them forever. The knowledge that they also won out because they were thinking men is as fine a reward as any of us could want."[7]

In 1949, Cobb married for the second time, in a small ceremony in Buffalo, New York. His bride was Frances Fairburn, the daughter of a longtime friend. Unlike Charlotte, Frances enjoyed the outdoors and the celebrity that came with being Ty Cobb's wife. She was 40 years old and Cobb was 62. In 1956, she too divorced Cobb, citing cruelty. Cobb's abrasive personality had cost him another marriage. In addition, unlike his playing days when he had avoided alcohol, Cobb drank heavily in retirement.

In his last decade, Cobb found comfort in using his wealth to help others. In 1950, in memory of his parents, Cobb contributed $100,000 for the creation of the Cobb Memorial Hospital in Royston. Over the years, the hospital grew into a full-blown healthcare system, serving thousands of miles of rural Georgia and employing more than 700 people. In 1953, Cobb established the Cobb Educational Foundation for needy students throughout Georgia. The foundation has awarded scholarships ranging from $150 to $20,000. In the 1996–1997 academic year, Cobb's foundation distributed nearly $500,000 to students.

In the decades following his baseball career, Cobb's money churned itself into a fortune. Estimates of his wealth range from five to ten million dollars at the time of his death. On occasions when he was admitted to the hospital, Cobb carried a bag filled with negotiable bonds and a pistol. He distrusted lawyers and handled his financial matters himself. Up to the last days of his life he made constant phone calls to traders, selling and buying stock.

As Cobb moved into his seventies, his health failed him. Late in 1959, while on a hiking trip with a friend near his home in Reno, Nevada, Cobb suffered an attack in the woods. "The pain almost paralyzed me and I found myself unable to walk," Cobb later told his friend, George Haines. His companion had to practically carry Cobb back to his house, a task that took several hours. Once they arrived at Cobb's home, Ty was placed in his bed but refused to accept treatment from a doctor, despite pain in his stomach and chest. This episode was described as "the beginning of his two-and-one-half year illness with crucial and almost unbearable pain." Shortly afterward, Frances Cobb, from whom he was divorced, took care of Ty for more than two weeks. She was able to convince Cobb to seek treatment from a doctor in California, which he did. Ultimately, he was diagnosed with Bright's disease, an inflammation of the kidneys.[8]

In 1960, Cobb's body began to fall apart. He spent several weeks in and out of hospitals, and relied on dozens of medications to alleviate the pain. He spent much of his time in bed, unable to move the legs that had touched home plate more times than any man in baseball history. As the end neared, Cobb scrambled to preserve his legacy, hiring sportswriter Al Stump to write his memoirs. Over the course of several months, Stump lived with Ty, taking notes and surviving the day-to-day drama that was Cobb's old age. As Cobb dictated a story about baseball and greatness, Stump focused on the bitter emptiness that was an old man's last gasp. Eventually, Stump published Cobb's autobiography, but he also wrote a shocking series of features that were considered grossly unfair to the baseball legend.

In his sessions with Stump, Cobb often fell into a melancholy stupor that was brought on in part by the prescription drugs and the alcohol he was consuming. A part of Cobb realized he had made mistakes in his life, and even questioned his career choice. "If I had my life to live over again, I would be a surgeon instead of a ball player," Cobb said, "I think I could have done a great deal of good in surgery. I would have been of some help to humanity."[9] But just as quickly, he would defend his style of play, recalling the infamous spiking of Frank Baker in 1908: "The base paths belonged to me, the runner. The rules gave me the right. I always went into a bag full speed, feet first. I had sharp spikes on my shoes. If the baseman stood where he had no business to be and got hurt, that was his fault."[10]

Cobb alternated between contentment and remorse in his final years. Sometimes, he was at ease with the life he had led: "Quite honestly, I can testify that I am not burdened with regrets. Would I play it the same way if I had a second chance? Yes, indeed, with an adjustment here and there." But on occasion he felt regret: "[M]aybe I went too far. I always had to be right in any argument I was in, and wanted to be first in everything. . . . I do indeed think I would have done things different. And if I had, I would have more friends."[11]

In April 1961, Cobb mustered the energy to travel to Los Angeles for the expansion-born Angels home opener. The Angels were managed by Fred Haney, Cobb's utility infielder from his 1920s Tigers. Cobb threw out the ceremonial first pitch at the last baseball game he ever attended.[12]

Less than two months later, Cobb was admitted to Emory Hospital in Atlanta. He kept the nurses and doctors who treated him on their toes with his spirited conduct. On one occasion, he threw his bedpan at an orderly who he thought had insulted him. Cobb remained in the hospital for the rest of life. It was there that he bitterly clung to the life he had led, unapologetic. "I had to fight all my life to survive," Cobb said, "They were all against me. But I beat the bastards and left them in the ditch."[13]

Cobb's health gradually deteriorated, prompting friends and family to rush to his bedside. He died on July 17, 1961, surrounded by his three surviving children and his first wife, Charlotte; he was 74 years old. That evening, Tigers broadcaster Ernie Harwell wrote this tribute that he read over the public address system at Navin Field, by then renamed Tiger Stadium, in Detroit:

> Baseball's greatest player—Tyrus Raymond Cobb—died today in his
> native Georgia. Cobb was a genius in spikes. His mind was the keen-

est ever to solve the strategy of the diamond. He was very fiery and dazzling on the base paths. For 24 years of high-tensioned baseball action, his name led all the rest. He was the best—in batting, base-stealing, run-making—in everything. Cobb's rise to fame in the early 1900s kept step with the progress of baseball as a national spectacle. His dynamic spirit was a symbol for the ever-growing industrial community he represented: Detroit, Michigan. And now, here in a baseball stadium where the cheers were the loudest and longest for this greatest of all Tigers, let us stand and pay final tribute to him in a moment of silence.

Two days later, close to 200 mourners attended Cobb's memorial service in Cornelia, Georgia, less than thirty miles from Royston. One misconception about Cobb's funeral that is often cited by critics to point out how hated he was, is that only three people from baseball attended the services. In actuality, the family organized a very private funeral, inviting members of the family and close personal friends. The Cobb family invited three baseball "officials" to attend: Mickey Cochrane, and single representatives from the American League and Commissioner's office. Cochrane, Nap Rucker, Cobb's old teammate from the Augusta Tourists, and Ray Schalk, who accompanied Cochrane, attended the services. Also in attendance was Sid Keener, an official from the Baseball Hall of Fame. Jimmy Cobb recalled that "the telegrams, letters, and cards we received from my father's friends, fans, and admirers from throughout the world would have filled many bushel baskets."[14]

Ty Cobb, the greatest and most feared player in the history of the game, was no more. He left behind a slew of records, including the most hits, runs scored, and stolen bases in baseball history. He also bequeathed a fortune to his family and his educational foundation. Later, Lou Brock, Pete Rose, and Rickey Henderson erased Cobb's career marks for hits, runs, and steals, but they couldn't diminish the greatness of the Georgia Peach. Cobb's career batting mark of .367 still towers as the greatest in history, and no other player has approached his twelve batting titles. He remains one of the most compelling athletes to ever grace the fields of competition.

NOTES

1. Broeg, *Superstars of Baseball*, 52.
2. Jerome Holtzman, *Memories and Dreams*, Fall 2003, 14.
3. Ibid., 15.
4. McCallum, *The Tiger Wore Spikes*, 131.

5. James C. Isaminger, *Sporting News*, October 4, 1928, 1.

6. *Sport Digest*, March 1989, 31.

7. Cobb, with Stump, *My Life in Baseball*, 258.

8. Ty Cobb file, National Baseball Hall of Fame Library.

9. *Sporting News*, July 5, 1950, 16.

10. Cobb, with Stump, *My Life in Baseball*, 69.

11. Ty Cobb file, National Baseball Hall of Fame Library.

12. Alexander, *Ty Cobb*, 234.

13. Ty Cobb file, National Baseball Hall of Fame Library.

14. *Sport Digest*, March 1989, 31.

Ty Cobb's Legacy

The death of Ty Cobb in 1961 served as a symbolic severing of ties with baseball's dead ball era. The man whom many considered baseball's greatest player, a man who had used the unique conditions of his time to his benefit on the diamond, was no longer alive to champion his way of play. That method of play was seemingly gone forever, with home runs being hit at a record pace in 1961. But within a few years, Cobb's name would resurface as one of his oldest records was broken.

In 1962, Maury Wills, a switch-hitting shortstop for the Los Angeles Dodgers, stole an amazing 104 bases. Wills' daring thievery recalled the days of Cobb and eclipsed Ty's record of 96 steals in 1915. With Wills and fellow National League speedster Lou Brock leading the way, the stolen base reemerged as an offensive weapon. Throughout the 1970s and into the 1980s, stolen bases continued to increase as teams found that they could hit home runs *and* run the bases with aggression. In 1977, Brock broke Cobb's career stolen base record, a record later pushed to new heights by Rickey Henderson. Henderson broke an even more important Cobb record in 2001 when he became baseball's all-time run scorer. For seventy-three years, Cobb had held the mark for touching home plate the most.

But the event that dragged Cobb's name into the headlines most prominently after his death was Pete Rose's assault on the all-time hits record. Cobb had banged out 4,191 hits in his twenty-four-year career,[1] a total unchallenged since his retirement. Such greats as Stan Musial and Hank Aaron had crept no closer than 420 hits from Cobb. Until Rose came along, it seemed Cobb's hit total was safe at the top of the charts.

In 1953, Cobb poses with three medallions to be given to the trustees of the Cobb Educational Foundation. © *Bettmann/CORBIS.*

But Pete Rose shared two traits with Cobb: he was determined and he was aggressive. Rose got as much out of his ability as any player in the history of the game. Although few would dispute that Cobb was a far better player than Rose (Rose hit .303 for his career, far below Cobb's .367 mark, and never once hit higher than .348 in a season), "Charlie Hustle" did take aim at Cobb's mark, catching him on September 11, 1985, with a single. Later, in 1989, when Rose was banned from baseball for a gambling scandal, another eerie parallel surfaced. Cobb had been embroiled in a gambling scandal of his own in 1926–1927, although he was exonerated and played two more seasons after the controversy.

With his all-time hit record erased, Cobb's playing legacy remained his overwhelming career batting mark of .367 and his 12 batting titles. In 1947, his friends at Coca-Cola, whose stock had made the former ballplayer tremendously wealthy, honored Cobb in their "All-Time Winners" poster series. The series introduced a new generation of fans to players like Cobb, golfing great Bobby Jones (a personal friend of Cobb), football star Red Grange, and boxing champion Gene Tunney. Other products continued to emerge over the years with Cobb's likeness, including the Corn States Serum Company calendar in the 1950s, which featured Cobb in a popular painting. In 1986, on the 100th anniversary of both Coca-Cola and Ty Cobb's birth, the soft drink giant issued a commemorative bottle with Cobb's photo and the words "Royston, Georgia Proudly Salutes the Immortal Ty Cobb, The Georgia Peach." The day after Cobb's death, Hillerich and Bradsby, the makers of Louisville Slugger bats, ran ads in six newspapers nationwide honoring their most famous customer. In part the ad read: "The World of Sport has lost its most spirited competitor. Baseball has lost its most brilliant player. We have lost a true friend."

Cobb's off-field persona underwent several attacks in the years following his death. The article "Ty Cobb's Wild, 10-Month Fight to Live," written by Al Stump, Cobb's biographer and confidant in his final days, was damning. Published originally in the December 1961 issue of *True: The Man's Magazine*, Stump's article largely portrayed Cobb as a bitter, alcoholic, psychotic old man. The author went so far as to speculate that Cobb was "emotionally disturbed," dating back to the days following his father's death.[2] The article chronicled Stump's ten-month collaboration with Cobb on the ballplayer's autobiography. On a friend's recommendation, Cobb chose Stump to author what he thought would become the greatest book on baseball ever written. Starting in the fall of 1960, Stump lived with Cobb practically nonstop, traveled with him, and was nearly killed by Cobb in a car accident. Severely medicated, Cobb made wild statements, such as claiming that he had killed one of his attackers back in Detroit in 1912, and that agents of the government were spying on him. While Stump wrote the book Cobb wanted, which was published a few months after Cobb's death, he also secretly took notes for another book, one that would exploit the intimate access Cobb had afforded him. Those notes blossomed into "Ty Cobb's Wild, 10-Month Fight to Live," which was immediately both popular and controversial.

Sportswriter Jack McDonald, a friend of Cobb's who had also seen Ty within the last few months of his life, reacted to Stump's article with venom. "This piece was written in poor taste by a man Ty had befriended. Some of the episodes described in it are gruesomely stomach-turning."[3] McDonald disputed Stump's claims that Cobb hit a woman in the nose with a baseball bat, used stamps sent to him by fans for his own mail, and drove like a maniac. Other Cobb friends chimed in as well. Pants Rowland, former American League umpire and manager during Cobb's playing days, disputed the claim that Cobb was emotionally disturbed as a player and remembered that he "never got any squawks from Cobb on balls and strikes." Rowland claimed, "Cobb was the greatest player of all time. But he was an individualist. And that was the basis of some of his unpopularity among his own teammates, such as Sam Crawford. But years later it was Cobb's efforts that helped to put Sam into the Hall of Fame."[4] Also coming to Cobb's defense were Ray Schalk and Red Faber, two opposing players who were Cobb admirers. "I loved the guy," Schalk said.[5]

Stump's most grievous injustice was in using the last dying breaths of a lonely man to characterize an entire life. Who among us can be judged solely by our actions during times of great stress? No greater stress can be thrown upon a man than the reality of his own mortality. Unfortunately, Stump ends his article with the legend of Cobb's funeral, which he says only three baseball men attended. But the story is apocryphal. In fact, several baseball figures wished to attend, but the family held a private ceremony.

Stump's portrait of Cobb became cemented in the minds of baseball fans even more in 1994, when Ron Shelton's feature-length film *Cobb* was released. The movie, starring Tommy Lee Jones in the title role, dealt almost exclusively with Cobb's last days, and relied on Stump's notes for the foundation of the story. In so doing, it ignored the charitable efforts Cobb had been involved in most of his life. The tagline for the film was "Everyone hated this baseball legend. And he loved it."[6] In fact, Cobb had friends, and he could be very sensitive. True, had he been easier to get along with, he would have gained more friends, but that fact was hardly lost on Cobb, and it weighed on his mind in his waning days. Shelton's depiction of Cobb was flat. It lacked the layers of complexity that made up Cobb. It also perpetuated the myth that the death of Cobb's father was the catalyst that pushed Ty into a rage from which he never retreated. In fact, Cobb had been a difficult man prior to his father's death, and although he had more than his share of confrontations, he was also a gentleman and a popular player, despite his transgressions. The film was a box office bust and was not widely released in theaters.

Cobb's reputation had suffered an earlier blow on the big screen in 1989's *Field of Dreams*, directed by Phil Alden Robinson. The film, starring Kevin Costner, is a fantasy about a farmer in Iowa who plows under his crops to build a baseball field in hopes that the ghost of Joe Jackson will return. Jackson does return, along with several other dead ballplayers, and when Cobb's name comes up, Jackson, played by Ray Liotta, says: "We thought about asking Cobb to come, but none of us could stand the son-of-a-bitch when he was alive, so we told him to stick it!" Ironically, the film treats the memory of Jackson, a player banned from baseball for life for throwing games during the 1919 World Series, better than it does Cobb.

Several biographers have taken their crack at the Cobb legend. The first serious work was Gene Schoor's *The Story of Ty Cobb: Baseball's Greatest Player*, published in 1952. John McCallum's *The Tiger Wore Spikes* followed in 1956. McCallum's book is far more valuable than Schoor's because it is filled with several stories that came directly from Cobb, with whom McCallum was a close friend. Of course, McCallum's friendship does warp his perspective, but the book remains a good look at how Cobb was viewed in the 1950s, and the stories contained within are some of the most enjoyable of Cobb's playing exploits.

Stump's book with Cobb, *My Life in Baseball, the True Record*, was published in 1961, just two months after Cobb's death. Written from Cobb's point-of-view, the book is noncontroversial, but it does give an insight into how Cobb perceived himself. In some parts, he is candid and critical of himself, but the underlying theme is of Cobb propping up his legacy. Still, the book is very good, and remains one of the best autobiographies in the sport. The real truth about Ty Cobb lies somewhere between the gloss of his autobiography, and the scathing article later written by Stump.

In 1984, Charles C. Alexander, a professor of history at Ohio University, produced the most complete and balanced biography on Cobb. In *Ty Cobb*, Alexander left no stone unturned, and took on every controversial subject and incident of Cobb's life with meticulous analysis. What emerges is a well-rounded picture of what Cobb was really like. Alexander resisted the temptation to characterize Cobb as nothing more than an angry racist. Instead, the book illustrates all facets of Cobb's life, relationships, and personality and remains the most in-depth study of Ty Cobb.

In 1994, Richard Bak's *Ty Cobb: His Tumultuous Life and Times* took its place as the best illustrated history of Cobb's life. With more than 180 pages of facts and photos, some of them rarely seen in print, Bak's book is a valuable edition to the study of Cobb. In 2002, Dr. William R. Cobb, a great-nephew, dusted off several articles written by Ty in the 1920s and self-published them as *Memoirs of Twenty Years in Baseball.* The articles are short and easy to read, dealing with subjects from how to bunt to details about Cobb's childhood.

In his 2002 novel, *Tyrus: An American Legend,* Patrick Creevy uses the death of Cobb's father as the basis for a fictionalized drama. Creevy's book is a breezy read with interesting dialogue and a compelling story. To be fair, Creevy makes no assertions that he is attempting a verbatim recreation of the events of W. H. Cobb's death and Amanda Cobb's trial. As a fictional story, the events are interesting and ironic. Ron Shelton may have been better served to write a movie based on Creevy's take of Cobb's life.

Cobb's name has proven to have iconic value over the years. In the closing credits of the popular 1970s sitcom *Welcome Back, Kotter,* a young woman is shown wearing a varsity jacket with "Ty Cobb Cheerleaders" on the front. The band Soundgarden had a song called "Ty Cobb" on its 1996 album *Down on the Upside.* In the late 1990s, a pop group from Philadelphia, described as producing "taut, jagged pop in the style of The Beatles, Guided by Voices, and BRMC,"7 took the name Ty Cobb for their band. The band members claimed to have decided on the name after seeing a trivia question in a bar that asked, "Who was the only player to beat up a fan with his own crutch?" The story is an obvious albeit inaccurate reference to the Claude Lueker incident in New York in 1912. In 2000, a stage play entitled *Cobb,* written by Lee Blessing, debuted off-Broadway. The play examined Cobb's life through actors portraying the ballplayer as a young man, as a middle-aged millionaire, and as a bitter, lonely old man. In addition, an actor portrayed Oscar Charleston, the Negro leaguer known as "the Black Ty Cobb." Charleston's character served as a stark reminder that players of Cobb's era never faced the best competition because of the racial segregation in baseball. The play received good reviews, and a version of it was performed at the Hall of Fame in Cooperstown, New York. Cobb's name has even popped up in David Letterman's Top Ten List. On the show that aired April 5, 1994, number 3 in Letterman's "Top Ten Ways the Mets Can Improve," was "Hire the ghost of Ty Cobb to hang around the dugout and give out kicks in the ass!"8

In Georgia, young people continue to benefit from Ty Cobb's generous philanthropy. Through July 2003, the Ty Cobb Educational Fund, which Cobb started in 1953, had awarded $9,743,000 in scholarships to more than 6,000 students throughout the "Peach State." The charter of the foundation states: "Although Ty Cobb's top annual salary as a baseball player was less than $40,000, his shrewd investments made him a financial success at an early age."9 Members of the board have included Brigadier General Fred W. Rankin, the Chief Consulting Surgeon of the United States Army during World War II, and a pioneer in surgical techniques; noted surgeon Daniel C. Elkin of Atlanta; Emory University President Harmon W. Caldwell; Major League Baseball Commissioner Albert "Happy" Chandler; and former player and Hall-of-Famer Earle Combs.

For several years, beginning immediately following Cobb's death, the people of Royston, Georgia, attempted to build a museum honoring their famous native son. For years the money trickled in here and there, with the Georgia State Legislature promising to provide funds once private donations were secured. Unfortunately, the effort was a long, uphill battle, filled with disappointment. In 1961, with the baseball world abuzz over Stump's behind-the-scenes article of Cobb's final days, Dr. Stewart Brown, Cobb's old teammate on the Royston Reds when both men were boys, explained how difficult it was to combat Stump's unfavorable image of Royston's most famous son. "It is inconceivable how a magazine can be allowed to print such material that would degrade the name and fame of Ty Cobb," Brown wrote in a letter to *Sporting News* publisher J. G. Taylor Spink. "I received a card from a Cobb fan in California, who, after reading the article, said that he would never contribute anything to a Cobb memorial."[10]

Eventually, in the late 1970s, the Joe A. Adams Professional Building in the Ty Cobb Memorial Healthcare System was assigned to house a library and small museum honoring Cobb. In the 1980s, the entire building was transformed into the Ty Cobb Museum, which today strives to fulfill the mission to "foster an appreciation for the life and career of Tyrus Raymond Cobb and his impact on the game of baseball by collecting, preserving, exhibiting, and interpreting artifacts related to Cobb for a local, regional and national audience."[11] Because most of Cobb's belongings were gifted to the National Baseball Hall of Fame while he was still alive, the museum in Royston houses few artifacts from his playing career. However, one notable exception is the medal Cobb was presented by Detroit fans for his first batting championship in 1907. For some time, a billboard greeted visitors to the small rural town with the message: "Welcome to Royston. Home of Baseball's Immortal Ty Cobb."

Despite his bad reputation, Cobb continued to stay near the top of nearly every expert's list of greatest players, long after his death. In 1987, the *Sporting News* selected him as one of their top five players of all time. In 1999, when Major League Baseball selected the All-Century Team, Cobb was picked to one of the outfield positions. In 2004, the 100th anniversary of Cobb's first professional baseball game (May 16, 1904, in Anniston, Alabama), Cobb's batting mark of .367 still towered over the baseball landscape as one of the sport's most unapproachable records. Historian and baseball statistics guru Bill James selected Cobb as the second greatest center fielder of all time behind Willie Mays, and even went out of his way to defend Cobb's tarnished image. "Ty Cobb's racism and his anger . . . were fueled not by smugness or even resentment, but by an unusually intense fear of his own limitations. . . . When Ty Cobb felt threatened he lashed out at the world. He felt threatened a lot—but as long as he wasn't challenged, he was a very nice man."[12] James' analysis jibes with Cobb's own stern warning to Stump: "If you and I are going to get along, don't increase my tension."[13]

The legacy of Tyrus Raymond Cobb will continue to morph as time goes by. In history, generally, the more years that pass, the more people are judged by their record, and by not their personality. For Cobb, this would prove to be beneficial. Few are still alive who saw him play, and generations of baseball fans have been indoctrinated with the idea that Cobb was little more than a racist thug, a notion perpetuated by Al Stump and Ron Shelton's unfair portrayals in print and film. The brilliant genius of the Georgia Peach, as reflected in his amazing baseball career and through his charitable foundation, is closer to the legacy that he and his father would have liked for the Cobb name. Ty Cobb, the man, deserves to be remembered as a complicated figure, with many sides to his personality, not simply as a caricature. Cobb the player takes a back seat to no one.

NOTES

1. Due to two disputed hits in Cobb's record, several sources adjusted his total down to 4,189 after his retirement. Yet, the official statisticians of Major League Baseball, Elias Stats, maintain his record at 4,191. Consequently, Cobb's career batting average is shown as either .367 or .366, depending on the source. When Rose collected his record-breaking hit on September 11, 1985, it was the 4,192nd of his career.

2. Al Stump, "Ty Cobb's Wild, 10-Month Fight to Live," *True: The Man's Magazine*, December 1961, 115.

3. Jack McDonald, "McDonald, Scribe-Pal, Takes Exception to Cobb Illness Yarn," *Sporting News*, December 6, 1961, 15.

4. Edgar Munzel, "Chi Quartet Shouts 'Foul' Over Effort to Smear Ty," *Sporting News*, December 20, 1961, 14.

5. Ibid.

6. See the Internet Movie Database at www.imdb.com.

7. See www.cdbaby.com/tycobb.

8. See www.davidletterman.com.

9. See www.tycobbfoundation.com.

10. Jack McDonald, "McDonald Scribe-Pal, Takes Exception to Cobb Illness Yarn," *Sporting News*, December 6, 1961, 15.

11. See www.tycobbfoundation.com.

12. Bill James, *The New Bill James Historical Baseball Abstract* (New York: Free Press, 2001), 722–723.

13. Stump, "Ty Cobb's Wild, 10-Month Fight to Live," 38.

APPENDIX: TY COBB'S CAREER AND WORLD SERIES STATISTICS

CAREER STATISTICS

Year	Club	League	G	AB	R	H	2B	3B	HR	RBI	BA	PO	A	E	FA
1904	Augusta	Sally Lg.	37	135	14	32	6	0	1	—	.237	62	9	4	.946
1904	Anniston	Tenn.-Ala.	37	149	23	45	5	9	0	—	.302	46	2	5	.906
1905	Augusta	Sally Lg.	103	411	60	134	13	4	1	—	.326	149	15	13	.927
1905	Detroit	American	41	150	19	36	6	0	1	—	.240	85	6	4	.958
1906	Detroit	American	98	350	45	112	13	7	1	—	.320	209	14	9	.961
1907	Detroit	American	150	605	97	212*	29	15	5	—	.350*	238	30	11	.961
1908	Detroit	American	150	581	88	188*	36*	20*	4	—	.324*	212	23*	14	.944
1909	Detroit	American	156	573	116*	216*	33	10	9*	—	.377*	222	24	14	.946
1910	Detroit	American	140	509	106*	196	36	13	8	—	.385*	300	18	14	.958
1911	Detroit	American	146	591	147*	248*	47*	24*	8	—	.420*	376*	24	18	.957
1912	Detroit	American	140	553	119	227*	30	23	7	—	.410*	324	21	22	.940
1913	Detroit	American	122	428	70	167	18	16	4	—	.390*	262	22	16	.947
1914	Detroit	American	97	345	69	127	22	11	2	—	.368*	177	8	10	.949
1915	Detroit	American	156	563	144*	208*	31	13	3	—	.369*	328	22	18	.951
1916	Detroit	American	145	542	113*	201	31	10	5	—	.371	335	18	17	.954
1917	Detroit	American	152	588*	107	225*	44*	23*	6	—	.383*	373	27	11	.973
1918	Detroit	American	111	421	83	161	19	14*	3	—	.382*	359	26	9	.977
1919	Detroit	American	124	497	92	191*	36	13	1	—	.383*	272	19	8	.973
1920	Detroit	American	112	428	86	143	28	8	2	63	.334	246	8	9	.966
1921	Detroit	American	128	507	124	197	37	16	12	101	.389	301	27	10	.970
1922	Detroit	American	137	526	99	211	42	16	4	99	.401	330	14	7	.980
1923	Detroit	American	145	556	103	189	40	7	6	88	.340	362	14	12	.969

Year	Club	League	G	AB	R	H	2B	3B	HR	RBI	BA	PO	A	E	FA
1924	Detroit	American	155	625	115	211	38	10	4	79	.338	417	12	6	.986
1925	Detroit	American	121	415	97	157	31	12	12	102	.378	267	10	15	.949
1926	Detroit	American	79	233	48	79	18	5	4	62	.339	109	4	6	.950
1927	Phil.	American	133	490	104	175	32	7	5	93	.357	243	9	8	.969
1928	Phil.	American	95	353	54	114	27	4	1	40	.323	154	7	6	.964
Major League Totals—24 years			3033	11429	2245	4191	724	297	117	727	.367	6501	407	274	.962
Minor League Totals—2 years			179	695	97	211	24	13	2	—	.304	257	26	22	.928

* indicates league leader

A = assists; AB = at-bats; BA = batting average; E = errors; FA = fielding average; G = games; H = hits; HR = home runs; PO = put-outs; R = runs; RBI = runs batted in; 2B = doubles; 3B = triples

WORLD SERIES RECORD

Year	Club	G	AB	R	H	2B	3B	HR	RBI	BA	PO	A	E	FA
1907	Detroit	5	20	1	4	0	1	0	0	.200	9	0	0	1.000
1908	Detroit	5	19	3	7	1	0	0	4	.368	3	0	2	.600
1909	Detroit	7	26	3	6	3	0	0	6	.231	8	0	1	.889
Totals, 3 years—		17	65	7	17	4	1	0	10	.262	20	0	3	.870

SELECTED BIBLIOGRAPHY

BIOGRAPHIES AND AUTOBIOGRAPHIES OF TY COBB

Alexander, Charles C. *Ty Cobb*. New York: Oxford University Press, 1984.

Bak, Richard. *Ty Cobb: His Tumultuous Life and Times*. Dallas: Taylor Publishing Company, 1994.

Cobb, Ty. *Memoirs of Twenty Years in Baseball*. Edited by William R. Cobb. Self-published by William R. Cobb, 2002.

Cobb, Ty, with Al Stump. *My Life in Baseball, the True Record*. New York: Doubleday and Company, 1961.

McCallum, John. *The Tiger Wore Spikes; an Informal Biography of Ty Cobb*. New York: A.S. Barnes and Company, 1956.

Schoor, Gene. *The Story of Ty Cobb, Baseball's Greatest Player*. New York: Messner, 1952.

Stump, Al. *Cobb: A Biography*. Chapel Hill, NC: Algonquin Books of Chapel Hill, 1994.

BOOKS

Alexander, Charles C. *John McGraw*. Lincoln: University of Nebraska Press, 1995.

Anderson, Dave. *Pennant Races: Baseball At Its Best*. New York: Galahad Books, 1997.

Bak, Richard. *Cobb Would Have Caught It: The Golden Age of Baseball In Detroit*. Detroit: Wayne State University Press, 1991.

Broeg, Bob. *Superstars of Baseball: Their Lives, Their Loves, Their Laughs, Their Laments*. South Bend, IN: Diamond Communications, 1994.

Creevy, Patrick. *Tyrus: An American Legend*. New York: Forge, 2002.

Curran, William. *Big Sticks: The Phenomenal Decade of Ruth, Gehrig, Cobb, and Hornsby.* New York: Harper Perennial, 1991.

Durso, Joseph. *Casey and Mr. McGraw.* St. Louis: The Sporting News, 1989.

Honig, Donald M. *Baseball When the Grass Was Real: Baseball from the Twenties to the Forties Told by the Men Who Played It.* New York: Coward, McCann and Geoghehan, 1975.

Kaplan, Jim. *Lefty Grove: American Original.* Cleveland: Society for American Baseball Research, 2000.

Levy, Alan H. *Rube Waddell: The Zany, Brilliant Life of a Strikeout Artist.* Jefferson, NC: McFarland and Company, 2000.

Lieb, Frederick G. *Connie Mack: Grand Old Man of Baseball.* New York: G. P. Putnam's Sons, 1945.

Okkonen, Marc. *The Ty Cobb Scrapbook: An Illustrated Chronology of Significant Dates In the 24-Year Career of the Fabled Georgia Peach, Over 800 Games From 1905 to 1928.* New York: Sterling Publishing Co., 2001.

Pietrusza, David. *Judge and Jury: The Life and Times of Judge Kenesaw Mountain Landis.* South Bend, IN: Diamond Communications, 1998.

ARTICLE

Stump, Al. "Ty Cobb's Wild, 10-Month Fight to Live." *True: The Man's Magazine,* December 1961, 38–41, 106–115.

MOVIES AND WEB SITES

Baseball history Web site (features profiles of many of the game's greatest players) www.thebaseballpage.com.

Cobb, VHS. Directed by Ron Shelton. Warner Bros., 1994. Tommy Lee Jones plays the role of Ty Cobb, and Robert Wuhl is biographer Al Stump. The film received poor reviews and was not widely released.

Field of Dreams. Directed by Phil Alden Robinson. Universal Studios, 1989. The cast includes Kevin Costner, Ray Liotta, James Earl Jones, Burt Lancaster, and Amy Madigan. The movie, which was based on the novel "Shoeless Joe," was nominated for an Academy Award for "Best Picture of the Year." The film is a fantasy about a farmer who plows under his crops to build a baseball diamond in hopes that Joe Jackson will return from the dead. At one point, the ghost of Shoeless Joe mentions Cobb briefly, stating: "We were going to invite Ty Cobb, but no one could stand the son-of-a-bitch when he was alive, so we told him to stick it!"

Grassroots organization Web site (dedicated to providing box scores for every major league game in history) www.retrosheet.org.

National Baseball Hall of Fame and Museum Web site: www.baseballhalloffame.org.

INDEX

About the Author

DAN HOLMES is Web Manager for the National Baseball Hall of Fame and Museum in Cooperstown, N.Y. He writes articles for the Hall of Fame Web site and publishes *Inside Pitch*, the Hall of Fame's weekly email newsletter.